Faith, Family
& the Feast

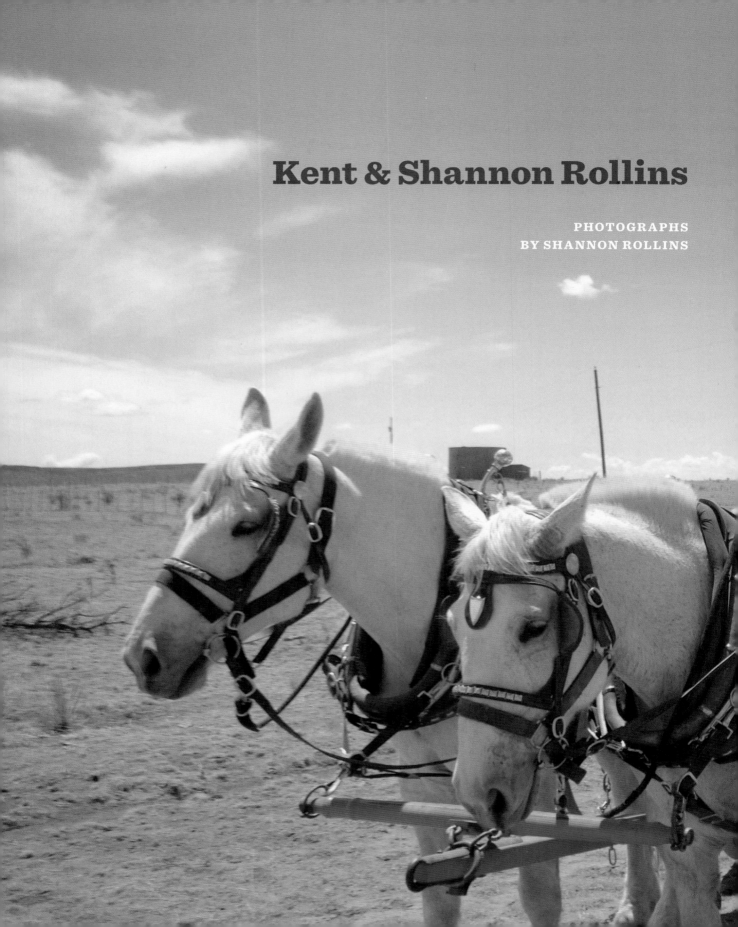

Kent & Shannon Rollins

PHOTOGRAPHS
BY SHANNON ROLLINS

Faith, Family & the Feast

Recipes to Feed Your Crew from the Grill, Garden, and Iron Skillet

A RUX MARTIN BOOK

HarperCollins Publishers
Boston New York

marinerbooks.com

Library of Congress Cataloging-in-Publication Data is available.

ISBN: 978-0-358-12449-8 (hbk); 978-0-358-12243-2 (ebk)

Book design by Melissa Lotfy

Printed in China
SCP 10 9 8 7 6 5 4 3 2
4500846675

DEDICATION

We dedicate this book to the little places, the ones you may have traveled through going somewhere else. Small towns across the nation that maybe time has passed by, but life is still there. Where Sunday socials after church offer not only five-star dining but, more importantly, fellowship. Where the coffee is served hot at community cafés and the conversations are always flowing. They may just seem like dots on a map, but we know these places are beacons of hope.

We dedicate this book to those feeding their families not only with food but with values and faith.

Finally, we dedicate this book to veterans and our servicemen and women. We are grateful for the sacrifices made by these individuals and families so that we may enjoy the freedoms we have in a country that we are blessed to live in. We tip our hats to you all.

Contents

Introduction

Have you ever seen a Norman Rockwell painting and wished you could have been transported to that place? Rockwell just seemed to have a knack for capturing the best of American life—its people and places. And for a minute you get a glimpse into a simpler time.

These scenes aren't a lost art, but they are fading. I was raised in such a place, and I'd like to invite y'all there. Where we live, hard work and values are more than just words—they are daily actions. Faith in God and family gets us through the hard times.

The world today is a busy place. So many families rely on fast food and even faster schedules. From emails to text messages, modern technology has nearly taken over. And here I was thinking that the Pony Express was a pretty brilliant invention—a feller on a horse with a letter is just my style of communication! It seems we're all so busy that we don't even have time for conversation. Folks hold a phone at the table rather than a fork. Why, if we're not careful, we're liable to end up with a drive-through window at my chuck wagon!

For those of you meeting my wife, Shannon, and me for the first time, let me introduce you to the lifestyle that we are blessed to lead. Shannon and I cook year-round, whether from our 1876 Studebaker chuck wagon feeding cowboys on working cattle ranches, firing up the grill in the backyard, or gathering with friends and family in the kitchen to celebrate a meal together.

When I first met Shannon while hosting a cooking workshop in her hometown of Elko, Nevada, she claimed to know nothing about cooking. I introduced her to the chuck wagon and taught her about cowboy and cast-iron cooking. Now she can dang near run the whole business with one finger. She's like American Express—I don't go anywhere without her. I've seen her lift Dutch ovens filled with food that nearly weigh as much as she does, split wood, drive a wagon, and cook a gourmet meal over a hot fire, no matter the weather or the time of day. There are no spa days or pedicures out here. She is often the first woman to have ever cooked off a chuck wagon at some of the ranches we've worked. She is also a great photographer, and all the pictures you'll find in this book are hers. From scenic views around camps and dusty pens of cattle to hungry cowboys and full plates of food, it takes someone special to capture a glimpse into our world.

The ranches and camps we cook for aren't fancy, but neither was our kitchen table when I was young, nor the food on it, but it did bring family and friends together. My mother used to say, "It's not the legs around this table that hold it up, but the family gathered at it." As Mama, Dad, my two older brothers, my sister, and I all sat together visiting, laughing, and eating, someone else always seemed to drop by for a visit. Mama was a great cook, and not only that, she could make a feast out of a few simple ingredients. There were no china plates nor fancy fixings, but neither was there such a thing as a Sunday social or Fourth of July celebration without her slow-churned homemade ice cream.

Before nearly every meal, Mama would say, "I taught you manners, God gave you grace, and we are going to use both at every meal!" I think she mainly meant that as a warning not to spill anything as we ate, but there's still a lot of weight in those words.

Just like at Mama's old kitchen table, Shannon and I try to make everyone feel welcomed wherever we're cooking, whether it's on a ranch or at home in our kitchen. It's a gathering place where stories are shared, the food is served up family style, and there's always enough for seconds.

Family nights on ranches are particularly special because those are times when the wives and children of the cowboys all come out. On longer ranch works, the fellers can be away from their families for several weeks, so it's a chance to reconnect and share a meal together. Before every meal, hats are removed since hands are clasped, and every head is bowed to say grace and offer thanks to the cow boss upstairs.

After the blessing, I yell, "Let's eat before I throw it out!" They fill their plates, find a spot to sit, and begin to discuss the day's hot topics. It might be about some unruly bovine, an ornery old horse, or what's coming up in the garden. All the cares of the modern world are set aside.

As farm and ranch folks, we have made our living from the things God has given us: fertile ground, rain, and sunshine. But most of all He gave us life, and I was taught to make the most out of life. No matter how bad it might seem, there is always something to be thankful for.

We wrote this book as a way to pass on the blessings we've received from living in a small rural cowboy community and to share the food, the stories, and the feeling of a happy heart. We wrote it to bear witness to all the things that I was fortunate to be raised around: garden ingredients, hot-off-the-grill goodness, and comfort foods sizzling in the old iron skillet. But this isn't just a cookbook, it's an open invitation to come spend time with us on the porch, visit, and set yourself a place at our table. So, praise the Lord—and pass the Jalapeño-Cheddar Buttermilk Biscuits!

A FEW TIPS FROM AN OLD HAND

Here we've compiled a few helpful tips to guide you through our book.

DEEP-FRYING

In recipes that call for deep-frying, choose an oil with a high smoke point, like canola or peanut oil. The best oil we've used is creamy liquid shortening, found in bulk at Sam's Club or Costco.

SKILLET AND DUTCH OVEN SIZING

You can easily swap a skillet or Dutch oven for a casserole dish and vice versa. Generally, a 9-x-13-inch casserole dish can be used in a recipe calling for a 12-inch cast-iron skillet or Dutch oven.

CERTIFIED ANGUS BEEF

We specifically look for the Certified Angus Beef brand—it's good every time. The main difference between it and other beef is marbling (the white specks of fat inside the meat). You want as much marbling as you can get because that's the secret to a mouthwatering steak. When you start with a lot of marbling, you don't need to dress it up more with fancy seasonings—it's just naturally tasty.

KNOW YOUR CHILES

Cowboy cooking is often influenced by traditional Mexican flavors, including chiles. You'll see several varieties of chiles used throughout this book.

Ancho chile: A sweet and smoky, mildly spicy dried chile. Guajillo chile can be substituted.

Cayenne chile: A moderately to highly spicy dried chile that adds heat and bite. Crushed red pepper flakes can be substituted.

Chile de árbol: Medium spicy, with a slight nutty, smoky flavor. Cayenne can be substituted.

Green chile: The best green chiles are Hatch chiles harvested in the Hatch Valley of New Mexico. Famous for their distinctive flavor, these chiles have a mild spiciness. Anaheim peppers, essentially the same but with a different flavor because they are not harvested in the same area, can be substituted. Hatch brand chiles can also be found in canned form.

Guajillo chile: A mild to medium-spicy dried chile. Slightly fruity, with a sweet heat. Cayenne pepper can be substituted, but it is spicier.

Serrano chile: Similar in flavor to a jalapeño, which can be substituted, but spicier.

Poblano chile: A moderately spicy chile; when dried is an ancho chile. Can be substituted with bell pepper, but won't have much spice.

Chipotle chiles: Smoked and dried jalapeños with a moderate to high spice level. They can often be found canned in an adobo sauce for an extra-smoky flavor plus added heat.

Burning Daylight

Breakfast

Sure, I set the alarm clock, but I'm always up before it goes off at 2:45 a.m. when I'm cooking for cowboys or ranch folks. It's time to start the day, 'cause those cowboys are counting on me. Whether your crew is a hungry bunch of cowboys, a houseful of kids, or the neighbors over for brunch, I bet you're like me, with everyone eagerly waiting on all the vittles you've prepared.

You might be asking, "Why so early?" Well, in the spring, depending on where we're camping, it begins to get light around 5 or 6 a.m., and it takes a while for bread to rise and coffee to boil.

As the fellers gather around the table, they'll pour themselves a cup of coffee and wait for me to give the call to eat: "Let's gather 'round, boys, it's time to bless it." Each one stands in reverence, with hat in hand and head bowed as we pray. We thank the good Lord for the blessings we have, the grace to get us through the day without any bad horse wrecks, and the opportunity to have another great one above the grass.

When the cowboys disperse for their morning chores before the break of dawn, they tip their hats and thank us. That's the best start to our day. As they leave to gather their horses, I hear the jingling of spurs in the distance. The sun begins to peek over the horizon, and I see the silhouettes of men and horses kicking up dust as they ride out in single file. I hear someone yell, "Let's hit a trot—we're burning daylight."

17

Breakfast Burritos with Salsa Verde

PREP TIME: **10 minutes**

TOTAL TIME: **35 minutes**

MAKES SIX TO EIGHT 8-INCH BURRITOS

Peanut or canola oil for frying

1½ cups peeled and chopped potatoes (russet or red)

1 pound ground sausage

½ large red bell pepper, chopped

½ large green bell pepper, chopped

1 medium yellow onion, chopped

5 large eggs

2 tablespoons mayonnaise

Salt and black pepper

6 to 8 (8-inch) flour tortillas (store-bought or homemade, page 110)

About 2 cups shredded cheddar cheese for topping

Salsa Verde (opposite)

We sure like burritos, because they're those grab-and-go meals. Mayonnaise, added to the whipped eggs, gives them a richer flavor, and, combined with sausage and peppers, sure will fill a feller up! We jazz up store-bought salsa verde with a little garlic and smoke to keep you full and in the saddle until noon. This will make six cowboy-sized burritos or around eight for normal folks.

1. In a large cast-iron skillet, heat 3 to 4 tablespoons oil over medium heat. Add the potatoes and cook, stirring occasionally, until lightly browned and tender, about 8 minutes. Remove from the skillet with a slotted spoon and drain on a paper towel.

2. Crumble the sausage into the same skillet and cook over medium-high heat, stirring occasionally. When it begins to brown, stir in the bell peppers and onion and continue to cook, stirring occasionally, until the meat has browned and the peppers and onion are tender, 8 to 10 minutes.

3. In a medium bowl, whisk together the eggs, mayonnaise, and salt and pepper to taste.

4. Stir the potatoes into the skillet, then pour in the eggs. Reduce the heat to medium and cook, stirring frequently, until the eggs are cooked through.

5. Spoon the egg mixture onto the tortillas and sprinkle with the cheese. Roll up and serve. Pour salsa verde inside or over the burritos, or use as a dipping sauce.

Salsa Verde

PREP TIME: 5 minutes
TOTAL TIME: 5 minutes
MAKES ABOUT 1½ CUPS

1 cup store-bought salsa verde

1 (4-ounce) can chopped green chiles

½ teaspoon lime juice

½ teaspoon garlic powder

¼ teaspoon red pepper flakes

¼ teaspoon liquid smoke

Salt and black pepper

Whisk all the ingredients together in a bowl until combined. Serve cold or at room temperature. The salsa verde can be refrigerated, covered, for up to 1 week.

Huevos Rancheros

PREP TIME: **5 minutes**
TOTAL TIME: **35 minutes**
MAKES 6 SERVINGS

4 Roma tomatoes

2 white onions

2 jalapeños

1 or 2 serrano chiles

6 garlic cloves, peeled

2 dried guajillo chiles, stemmed, seeded, and finely chopped

Salt and black pepper

8 tablespoons bacon grease or vegetable oil

6 corn tortillas

6 large eggs

1 cup shredded queso fresco for sprinkling

Also known as Rancher's Eggs, this breakfast was a staple in camp when I was guiding elk hunters in the Gila Wilderness and has been a hit at our table ever since. The sauce is thick and spicy, with fresh and dried chiles and a flavor you sure won't find in a can. It's very versatile, and it will make enough to use as a salsa in other dishes.

---

1. Core the tomatoes. Slice the onions in half but leave the root ends intact until after boiling.

2. Add the tomatoes, onions, jalapeños, serranos, and 4 of the garlic cloves to a large saucepan and cover with water. Bring to a boil and boil for about 15 minutes, or until the tomatoes are tender, adding more water if needed.

3. Drain the vegetables and let cool. Soak the tomatoes in cold water for 2 to 3 minutes to make it easier to loosen their skins. Slip off the skins of the tomatoes and discard. Remove the stems and, if desired, the seeds from the jalapeños and serranos. Cut off the root ends of the onions.

4. Transfer all the vegetables to a blender and add the remaining 2 garlic cloves and the guajillos. Blend until smooth. Season with salt and pepper to taste.

5. Pour the contents of the blender into a medium saucepan and bring to a boil. Reduce the heat to a simmer, cover, and continue to cook for 10 minutes to incorporate the flavors, stirring occasionally.

6. Meanwhile, heat about 1 tablespoon of the bacon grease or oil in a medium cast-iron skillet over medium heat. Add a tortilla and turn to coat on both sides, then cook until it bubbles up slightly and warms through on both sides,

TIP

Make the sauce the night
before and refrigerate it for
a quick meal in the morning.
Rewarm the sauce before
serving. The sauce can
be stored, covered and
refrigerated, for up to 1 week.

45 seconds to 1 minute per side. Be sure not to overcook or it will become too crispy. Wrap in a towel to keep warm and repeat with the remaining tortillas, adding about 1 table-spoon bacon grease or oil for each one.

7. Add 1 tablespoon of grease to the skillet and fry half the eggs over easy, 1½ to 2 minutes. Repeat with the remaining eggs and 1 tablespoon grease.

8. Place the tortillas on plates, top with the eggs, sprinkle with a bit of the cheese, and drizzle each with a spoonful of the sauce. Top with more cheese, if desired. Serve immediately.

You will seek me and find me, when you seek me with all your heart.

— Jeremiah 29:13

Cowboy Eggs Benedict

PREP TIME: **25 minutes**
TOTAL TIME: **35 minutes**
MAKES 6 SERVINGS

4 slices thick-cut bacon

6 large eggs, at room temperature

2 store-bought piecrusts

1 cup shredded cheddar cheese

Peanut or canola oil for frying

Lemon Hollandaise Sauce (opposite)

Before you get too far into this, don't be thinking this is like the traditional restaurant-style eggs Benedict. This is cowboy style. First off, we're starting with a soft-boiled egg rather than a poached one, which is then wrapped in pie dough, along with crumbled bacon and cheese. Now deep-fry that rascal and smother it with our rich and smoky Lemon Hollandaise Sauce.

1. Cook the bacon in a medium skillet over medium-high heat until crispy. Drain on paper towels and let cool, then crumble or chop.

2. In a medium saucepan, cover the eggs with water, bring to a boil, and boil for 4½ minutes. Immediately remove the eggs from the water and place them in ice water for 4 minutes.

3. Meanwhile, roll out the piecrusts and cut out six 5- to 6-inch circles. Sprinkle each circle evenly with the crumbled bacon and shredded cheese. Set aside.

4. Tap each end of an egg lightly with a spoon to crack. Carefully peel the ends off. Slip a spoon under the shell and gently peel off the shell, or peel with your fingers. Be careful not to puncture the egg. Repeat with the remaining eggs.

5. Place an egg in the center of a dough circle. Wrap the dough around the egg and crimp together to seal. Repeat with the remaining eggs and dough.

6. In a large saucepan or Dutch oven, heat 3 to 4 inches of oil to 350°F. Add the eggs and deep-fry, turning in the oil, until golden brown, about 3 minutes. Remove with a slotted spoon and drain on paper towels or a wire rack before serving with the hollandaise sauce.

Lemon Hollandaise Sauce

PREP TIME: 5 minutes

TOTAL TIME: 5 minutes

MAKES ABOUT 1 CUP

2 large egg yolks

2 teaspoons lemon juice

½ teaspoon dry mustard

½ teaspoon paprika or smoked paprika

Pinch of red pepper flakes

Pinch of salt

1 stick butter, melted

1. In a small heatproof bowl, whisk together the egg yolks, lemon juice, mustard, paprika, red pepper flakes, and salt. Set up a double boiler by placing the bowl over a smaller saucepan of boiling water to where the bowl isn't touching the water. Whisk until smooth.

2. Still over the double boiler, slowly whisk in the butter and continue whisking until the sauce thickens, about 3 minutes. Serve immediately over the Cowboy Eggs Benedict.

TIP

If the sauce begins to thicken too much before serving, add 1 teaspoon hot water at a time until it reaches the desired consistency.

Fiesta Ranch Pizza

PREP TIME: **15 minutes**
TOTAL TIME: **40 minutes**
MAKES ONE 12-INCH PIZZA

3 large eggs

1 tablespoon mayonnaise

½ green bell pepper, chopped

Salt and black pepper

1 (12-inch) pizza crust (opposite)

⅓ cup store-bought ranch dressing

½ cup refried beans (store-bought or Ranch Refried Beans, page 143), warmed slightly

1 cup shredded cheddar cheese

Who doesn't like pizza for breakfast? Instead of pulling out that cold one from the night before, let's do something fresh. We start with eggs, of course, and some green bell peppers, but we also combine two ingredients that you might not think of for breakfast: ranch dressing and refried beans. Trust us: This will get you over your siesta and into fiesta mode!

1. Preheat the oven to 400°F with a rack in the middle.

2. In a medium bowl, whisk together the eggs, mayonnaise, bell pepper, and salt and pepper to taste.

3. Place the pizza crust on a baking sheet or baking stone. Be sure the lip of your crust is high enough to hold in the egg mixture.

4. Spread an even layer of the ranch dressing on the crust, followed by the beans. Carefully pour the egg mixture evenly on top. Sprinkle with the cheese.

5. Bake for 20 to 25 minutes, until the eggs are cooked through and the crust is browned on the bottom. Serve.

OUTDOOR COOKING TIP

Pizza is easy to cook in a Dutch oven. You can slip a fork under the crust and slightly pull up to see how the bottom is browning and adjust your heat as needed.

1 (¼-ounce) package active
dry yeast

1 cup warm water

2 teaspoons sugar

2 tablespoons olive oil

1½ teaspoons garlic salt or
onion salt

2¼ cups all-purpose flour,
plus more for dusting

Pizza Crust

1. In a medium bowl, whisk together the yeast, warm water and sugar until dissolved. Let sit until the mixture becomes bubbly, about 10 minutes.

2. Whisk in the olive oil and garlic salt. Slowly stir in the flour until combined. With your hands, lightly knead the dough around the bowl for 1 minute, adding more flour if the dough is too sticky. Cover and let rest for about 5 minutes.

3. Turn the dough out onto a lightly floured surface and knead it a few times to lightly coat the outside with flour and remove any stickiness, if needed.

4. Roll the dough out to a 16-inch circle (for a 14-inch pizza) or a 14-inch circle (for a 12-inch pizza). Fold the edge over all around to create a high lip to contain the filling.

TIP

You can also roll out the dough into a rectangle and bake the pizza on a baking sheet. This crust will bake up to about ½-inch thick when making a 14-inch pizza. If you like a thinner crust, roll the dough out thinly, cut and discard the excess.

Faith is believing in something that you can't see, but always having sight of it.

A Guiding Light

It was so cold that I could barely hold the match still as I tried to light the lantern that morning. My hands were shaking, and there was a stiff north breeze coming under the fly of the wagon. It felt like there was nothing between me and the Canadian border.

Every time I'd try to turn the knob to light the lantern, the match would be blown out. But finally, there was light. A small beacon of encouragement on this frigid twenty-first day of December, at 3:45 in the morning in the Palo Duro Canyon in Texas. I don't know the actual temperature, but I do know the water barrel was frozen solid, and I had to chop ice to make coffee.

Then the lantern went out again.

So back at it, with trembling hands and a match, I asked, "God, let there be light, I just need a little help. Those boys are depending on me for nourishment and warmth before they go off to do bovine battle."

And then, it was a small Christmas miracle, as the first match struck home and there I was, back in business. I stoked ol' Bertha, my wood stove, full of mesquite knots and slid the coffee pot over to let her work her magic. I pulled up an old canvas chair next to the stove and said, "Thank you, Lord, for the heat and the light."

So many mornings had started out this way, but something about this one seemed different. It was at about that moment when the howling winter's breath suddenly stopped. It was like someone shut the north door, and all I could hear was the crackling of embers inside Bertha as she began to come to life. As I soaked in the stove's warmth, I felt a calmness come over me. It was a familiar feeling, a feeling of hope, love, light.

It was then I remembered a Christmas message that I had heard at church, and I understood it better than I had some forty-five years ago. It too was about a cold night that started with a light. A guiding light and

a beacon of a new beginning. This light drew travelers in from afar, and there they found a small child lying in a manger. This child brought hope. This child brought peace.

The men who came to see the newborn child so long ago came bearing gifts. Well, the fellers who are drawn to the light of camp bring a gift as well, the gift of friendship. And even though those who visited the small child were dressed as wise men and shepherds, the men in my camp dressed as cowboys are wise too, because we all chose to follow.

I needed light that night. Light to see, light to begin. I doubted if that lantern would ever light, or if the wind would ever quit. I asked God for a little help, and He did, and He has ever since.

Ham-and-Egg Cast-Iron Quiche

PREP TIME: **10 minutes**
TOTAL TIME: **1 hour**
MAKES ABOUT 6 SERVINGS

1 store-bought piecrust

4 large eggs

2 cups heavy cream

1½ cups chopped ham

1 cup shredded cheddar cheese

⅓ cup chopped yellow onion

1 teaspoon salt

½ teaspoon black pepper

Don't worry: If you're like me and have never made a quiche, it's actually simple. It's basically a savory ham-and-egg bake in a flaky piecrust. Eggs are whipped up with cream, ham, and onion. But you can also incorporate your own favorite items in the filling for a new take on breakfast.

———◆◆———

1. Preheat the oven to 425°F. Butter a 9-inch deep-dish pie pan or an 8- to 10-inch cast-iron skillet.

2. Roll the piecrust out to a 12-inch diameter and fit it into the pan or skillet.

3. In a medium bowl, whisk together the eggs, cream, ham, cheese, onion, salt, and pepper. Pour into the piecrust and bake for 15 minutes.

4. Turn the oven down to 325°F and bake for another 35 minutes, or until the eggs have set and an inserted knife comes out clean. Let sit for about 5 minutes before serving.

TIP

You may need to cover the edge of the piecrust with foil while baking to prevent it from browning too quickly.

The road may not always be smooth, but it's worth the ride.

Ham, Egg, and Bacon Waffle Bake

PREP TIME: **15 minutes**

TOTAL TIME: **1 hour**

MAKES ABOUT 8 SERVINGS

6 slices thick-cut bacon, chopped into bite-sized pieces

1 stick butter, melted

6 to 7 frozen waffles, slightly thawed

6 large eggs

¼ cup mayonnaise

1½ cups heavy cream

Salt and black pepper

1 cup chopped ham

2 (2.75-ounce) packets gravy mix

1 cup water

You know when you go to your favorite coffee shop and wish you could have one of everything on the menu? I came up with this recipe 'cause it has all your favorites in one pan: waffles, bacon, eggs, ham, and gravy. It's convenient and also makes a great Dutch oven breakfast dish while camping.

---

1. Preheat the oven to 350°F.

2. In a medium skillet, cook the bacon over medium-high heat until about half to three-quarters done. Drain on a paper towel.

3. Pour half the butter into a 9-x-13-inch casserole dish or 12-inch cast-iron skillet and rotate around to lightly coat the bottom of the dish or skillet. Place the waffles at the bottom and tear any pieces and arrange to create an even single layer. Pour the remaining butter on top.

4. In a small bowl, whisk together the eggs, mayonnaise, and ½ cup of the cream. Season with salt and pepper to taste.

5. Evenly sprinkle the waffles with the bacon and ham, then pour the eggs on top.

6. In another small bowl, whisk together the gravy mix, water, and remaining 1 cup cream until smooth. Pour over the waffles.

7. Bake for about 40 to 45 minutes, or until the eggs are set and the top of the casserole is lightly browned. Serve.

OUTDOOR COOKING TIP

The bottom crust doesn't need to cook long. When the waffles puff up and release slightly from the side of the Dutch oven, you can take the oven off the bottom heat. Continue cooking with the top heat until the eggs are set and the top is lightly browned.

Three-Meat Hearty Hash

PREP TIME: **10 minutes**
TOTAL TIME: **35 minutes**
MAKES 4 SERVINGS

4 slices thick-cut bacon, cut into 1-inch pieces

4 ounces ground chorizo or spicy sausage

1 cup diced ham

1 poblano chile, chopped

½ yellow onion, chopped

1 garlic clove, minced

3 tablespoons peanut or canola oil

3 red potatoes, unpeeled, chopped

1 tablespoon butter

4 large eggs

Chopped green onion and shredded cheddar or pepper jack cheese for serving (optional)

My personal requirement for a good cowboy hash is meat—and a lot of it. For my win on Food Network's Cutthroat Kitchen, *during a breakfast-hash challenge I created a blend of crispy bacon, ham, and spicy chorizo. I also added a poblano chile for a smoky bite and topped it with over-easy eggs. Well, folks, I had it ready by the time show host Alton Brown hollered, "You better hurry, time is running out!"*

—◆—

1. In a large cast-iron skillet, begin browning the bacon over medium-high heat. When it's about three-quarters done, add the chorizo and stir to break it up.

2. When the chorizo has nearly cooked through, add the ham, poblano, and onion and continue to cook, stirring occasionally, until the vegetables are tender, about 5 minutes. Add the garlic and cook for another 1 to 2 minutes, stirring occasionally. Set aside.

3. Heat the oil in medium cast-iron skillet over medium-high heat. Add the potatoes and cook, stirring occasionally, until golden brown and tender, about 8 minutes. Drain any excess grease and add the potatoes to the large skillet with the chorizo.

4. Wipe out the skillet in which you cooked the potatoes and melt the butter over medium heat. Add the eggs and fry them over easy, 1½ to 2 minutes.

5. Divide the hash among four plates and place an egg on top of each serving. Top with green onion and cheese, if desired. Serve immediately.

Chile Relleno Breakfast Casserole

PREP TIME: **10 minutes**

TOTAL TIME: **1 hour and 5 minutes**

MAKES ABOUT **6 SERVINGS**

5 (4-ounce) cans whole green chiles

2 cups (about 14 ounces) cooked chorizo or spicy sausage, chopped

2 cups shredded Mexican blend cheese (see Tip)

4 large eggs

1 cup milk

¼ cup all-purpose flour

¾ cup red enchilada sauce (store-bought or homemade, page 202)

I just love a one-dish breakfast. It makes for an easier morning, and with this one, you sure aren't skimping on quality or that good homemade flavor. A layer of whole green chiles is topped with whisked eggs, chorizo, and lots of cheese. A bold red enchilada sauce finishes it all off.

1. Preheat the oven to 325°F. Lightly butter a 9-x-13-inch casserole dish or 12-inch cast-iron skillet.

2. Cut down one side of the chiles, roll them out to open, then layer them on the bottom of the casserole dish or skillet.

3. Top the chiles with the chorizo, then evenly sprinkle on 1½ cups of the cheese.

4. In a small bowl, whisk together the eggs, milk, and flour. Pour the mixture over the cheese.

5. Bake for about 45 minutes, until the eggs are set. Remove from the oven, top with the enchilada sauce, and sprinkle with the remaining ½ cup cheese. Bake for another 10 minutes, or until the sauce has warmed through. Serve.

TIP

Use any cheese blend of your choice, like cheddar and mozzarella.

Coconut French Toast

PREP TIME: **10 minutes**
TOTAL TIME: **25 minutes**
MAKES 6 SERVINGS

5 large eggs

⅔ cup milk

1 teaspoon ground cinnamon

1 cup all-purpose flour

1 cup shredded sweetened coconut

½ cup sugar

¾ to 1 stick butter for cooking

12 slices Texas toast or other thick-cut bread

Maple syrup for serving

The only time you should look down on someone is when you bend over to help them up.

Here in southwest Oklahoma, we love us some coconut! Shan would always tease me that my family would try to sneak coconut into every recipe we could. To satisfy my cravings, she came up with this recipe. It's easy and revives that ol' French toast recipe. Her version soaks a thick-cut slice of bread in the egg batter first, then dredges it through a sugary coconut and flour mixture before frying. This extra coating gives it a little more depth, with a light crust of coconutty goodness.

1. In a shallow dish, whisk together the eggs, milk, and cinnamon.

2. In another shallow dish, combine the flour, coconut, and sugar.

3. Heat a large skillet over medium-high heat. Add 1 tablespoon of the butter.

4. Working with 2 bread slices at a time, soak both sides of the bread slices well in the egg mixture, then dredge through the flour mixture. Pat the flour mixture onto the bread on both sides. Lightly shake off any excess flour from the bread and add them to the skillet.

5. Cook for 1 to 2 minutes per side, until lightly browned. Repeat with the remaining bread slices, adding about 1 tablespoon of the butter to the skillet per batch. Serve warm with syrup.

Pumpkin Pie Pancakes

PREP TIME: **5 minutes**

TOTAL TIME: **15 minutes**

MAKES ABOUT 10 PANCAKES

1 cup all-purpose flour

2 tablespoons sugar

2 teaspoons baking powder

½ teaspoon salt

½ teaspoon ground cinnamon

½ teaspoon ground nutmeg

¼ teaspoon ground cloves

1 cup milk

1 large egg

¼ cup canned pure pumpkin

1 teaspoon vanilla extract

1 to 2 tablespoons butter, or more as needed

Maple–Cream Cheese Syrup (below) or other maple syrup

I'd eat these nearly anytime, for any meal—and not just in the fall. I've got to give the credit to Shannon on this one because she came up with it. She knows I have a weakness for pancakes, but this recipe gives them a whole new twist. They come out of the skillet light and fluffy, with that classic taste of pumpkin mixed with cinnamon and cloves. They go perfectly with her smooth Maple–Cream Cheese Syrup. Avoid using pumpkin pie filling mix, which is sweetened and spiced; look for pure pumpkin filling.

1. In a large bowl, combine the flour, sugar, baking powder, salt, cinnamon, nutmeg, and cloves.

2. Whisk in the milk and egg, followed by the pumpkin and vanilla. Continue whisking until smooth.

3. Heat 1 tablespoon butter in a large skillet over medium heat for each batch of 5 pancakes. Pour about ¼ cup of the batter into the skillet for each pancake. Cook for 1 to 2 minutes per side, until golden brown and cooked through. Serve with Maple–Cream Cheese Syrup or your favorite syrup.

PREP TIME: 8 minutes

TOTAL TIME: 8 minutes

MAKES ABOUT 2 CUPS

1 (8-ounce) package cream cheese, softened

¼ cup milk

½ cup maple syrup

Maple–Cream Cheese Syrup

1. In a small saucepan, begin heating the cheese over medium-low heat, whisking until smooth.

2. Whisk in the milk and syrup and cook, whisking frequently, for about 3 minutes, or just until smooth and beginning to bubble. Serve warm over the pancakes.

The Dust of Our Fathers

I was raised and still live in the very southwest corner of Oklahoma, and if you throw a rock to the west, it will land in Texas. Our community of Hollis is nestled on a flat grassy prairie of the Great Plains. Wheat and cotton fields dot the landscape as well as cattle ranches, many of which have been in operation for generations.

It's harsh country. The wind blows, and the dust rolls here. Some calves are born and won't feel a raindrop on their backs for months. Folks don't just have grit in their teeth but in their hearts too. It's not for the weak, and most of the folks who call this their home are the descendants of Dust Bowl survivors.

Historians claim that the Oklahoma Panhandle was the epicenter of the Dust Bowl, and as the crow flies, Hollis is about 140 miles southeast of the panhandle. There were reports of the dirt traveling as far as New York City from the great dust storms in the 1930s, so really, our little town wasn't a far commute for the chaos to come knocking at folks' doors.

My father lived through the Dust Bowl in Hollis, along with his parents and four siblings. When I was growing up, he would tell us kids stories about the great darkness that swept over his home and as far as the eye could see when he was a little boy.

Remembering his tales now, I realize that he was not only part of the Greatest Generation but the toughest one as well. I can still hear his words today:

I remember the wind blowing pretty hard that first morning, which was the beginning of the Dirty Thirties. The sun disappeared like a storm was rolling in. But the clouds had a strange color to them. I asked Mama if it was a tornado. She seemed panicked and she called for us to come inside. The murky clouds kept building and tumbling over and over. I remember when the black wall finally hit—it was like a dark shadow laid itself over the house. Its evil breath full of dirt blew heavy against our door.

Mama lit a coal lantern in the kitchen even though it was early afternoon, when the sun should have still been shining. The wind beat on the house with an eerie howl, rattling the windowpanes so hard I thought they would shatter. Small particles of the earth crept into every crack of the house. Mama quickly hung quilts over the windows and doors, trying to keep the dust out. The wind went on for hours, and the coal lanterns grew dim from all the dust floating around us.

What we thought was just a bad storm that would last a few hours didn't leave. It stayed for six more years.

At night when Mama would put my twin sister and me to bed, she'd wrap our faces with a wet towel to keep us from breathing in the dust while we slept. I'd think, I can't go to sleep 'cause I might not ever get up. In the mornings, the wind would usually be calm, but it had left a calling

card. Across our white bedsheets were long, thin lines of dirt eight inches apart that had blown in through the cracks in the walls. Every few days, Pa and my older brothers would go up to the attic with a shovel to remove all the dirt to keep the ceiling from caving in. Chickens would roost in the middle of the day because of the darkness. Mailboxes were covered by sand drifts.

We called it the Devil's Breath. There was no escaping it. Everyone was affected—the rich, the poor, livestock. We'd go over to the neighbors' to help them remove some of their cows that had died from suffocation. Later, even more perished from starvation.

Even though that dark era is decades behind us, its presence still lingers in the areas where the heavy dirt settled throughout America's heartland. It's bred into its people. There's an undying faith that tomorrow will be better, there ain't no giving up, and always look for the good. The glass is always half full, so let's keep pouring! Faith, family, and courage got those folks through the toughest of times.

Like a sandblaster, the Dust Bowl removed a lot of things from this old country and her people, but it didn't get their will to survive. With a gritty force, it carved out a tougher, more determined bunch of folks.

I'm glad I didn't have to go through it, but I'm so proud and indebted to those who did. I hope to continue their legacy. So, when it hasn't rained in months and the wind kicks up the dust without ceasing, I remember how it must have been for my father and all our fathers who endured the hard times of the '30s, and I'll be thankful for the little bit of grit in my teeth and hope in my heart.

Dutch Baby with Mixed Berries

PREP TIME: **10 minutes**

TOTAL TIME: **35 minutes**

ABOUT 4 SERVINGS

3 large eggs

½ cup milk

¾ cup all-purpose flour

1 tablespoon granulated sugar

¼ teaspoon salt

1 teaspoon vanilla extract

1 teaspoon ground ginger

2 tablespoons butter

Butter, powdered sugar, berries, and/or syrup for serving (optional)

A classic cast-iron dish, a Dutch baby is a German-style pancake. It puffs up while baking and is a great sweet treat for breakfast . . . or that word Shan uses—brunch (I just call that sleeping in late). What gives this one its flavor is the addition of ground ginger. You can serve the pancake up with syrup, jam, or butter. Our favorite way is topped with powdered sugar and a mess of mixed berries!

———— •••• ————

1. Preheat the oven to 400°F with a rack in the middle.

2. In a medium bowl, whisk together the eggs and milk.

3. In another medium bowl, combine the flour, granulated sugar, and salt. Whisk the flour mixture into the egg mixture until smooth. Whisk in the vanilla and ginger.

4. Melt the butter in a 10-inch cast-iron skillet over medium-high heat. Remove from the heat and swirl the butter around to coat the skillet. Pour the excess butter into the batter and stir, then pour the batter into the hot skillet.

5. Bake for 20 to 25 minutes, until the pancake is puffed and golden brown along the edge. (The shorter cooking time will give you a softer pancake.)

6. With a spatula, carefully remove the Dutch baby from the skillet and let cool slightly on a wire rack before serving. Top with butter, powdered sugar, berries, and/or syrup as desired.

Best-Ever Crispy Hash Browns

PREP TIME: **10 minutes**
TOTAL TIME: **18 minutes**
MAKES ABOUT 2 SERVINGS

1 large russet potato, peeled

2 tablespoons clarified butter (see opposite) or store-bought ghee

Salt and black pepper

When it comes to good hash browns, everyone has the same rule: They have to be crispy! First you have to use a russet (baking) potato, because the higher starch content helps with the crispness. You'll need to rinse the potatoes before cooking, until the water comes clear. Be sure to use a cloth towel instead of paper towels when blotting the taters dry, because it absorbs more moisture. We use clarified butter because it doesn't burn on high heat as ordinary butter would and because it has a richer flavor. Finally, go find that lid for the skillet, which will ensure even cooking. Okay, let's get the skillet hot and get to it!

1. Shred the potato into a bowl of water. Stir the shredded potato around in the bowl, drain the water off, then add fresh water to cover. Repeat three or four times, until the water is clear.

2. With your hands, squeeze some of the water from the shredded potato and place it on a clean cloth towel. Fold the towel over and press down on the potato to remove excess water. Fluff the shredded potato with your hands, fold the towel over, and press out the moisture one more time.

3. Heat a large cast-iron skillet over medium-high heat. Add the clarified butter. When it just begins to bubble, bunch the grated potato together to form 2 pancakes in the skillet. Pat it down slightly. Season with salt and pepper to taste.

4. Cover the skillet and cook for about 5 minutes, until the pancakes begin to brown around the edges.

5. Flip and continue cooking without the lid for 2 to 3 minutes, until golden brown. Serve hot.

How to Clarify Butter

1. Slowly melt a stick of butter in a small saucepan over medium-low heat. Do not stir.

2. Once the butter is completely melted, a foamy white layer will form on top. Use a spoon to skim the foam off the top.

3. Remove from the heat and let sit for 5 minutes.

4. Strain the butter through cheesecloth or a coffee filter into a sealable container. The butter can be refrigerated for 4 to 6 months. Makes about 6 tablespoons of clarified butter.

Fried Cream of Wheat with Caramel-Pecan Syrup

PREP TIME: **2 hours and 15 minutes**
TOTAL TIME: **2 hours and 25 minutes**
MAKES ABOUT 6 SERVINGS

6 cups water

1 teaspoon salt

1¼ cups Cream of Wheat cereal

6 to 8 tablespoons bacon grease or butter for frying

Caramel-Pecan Syrup (opposite)

Traditionally, this warm and filling breakfast is made with cornmeal, but we're redoing it with Cream of Wheat. Cooked, chilled, cut into slices, and fried to crispness in good bacon grease, it becomes the perfect vehicle for the warm caramel syrup with chunks of pecans. You can also fry it in butter, but the bacon grease adds more flavor.

1. Bring the water and salt to a boil in a medium saucepan. Add the Cream of Wheat, reduce the heat to a simmer, and cook, stirring frequently, for 2 to 3 minutes, until thickened. Remove from the heat and let cool slightly.

2. Meanwhile, butter a 9-x-5-inch loaf pan. Pour the cereal into the pan and let cool for about 10 minutes. Cover and refrigerate for about 2 hours, until firm.

3. Run a knife around the edges and turn the cooled Cream of Wheat out of the pan. Cut into twelve ½- to ¾-inch-thick slices.

4. Heat about 1 tablespoon of the bacon grease over medium-high heat in a large cast-iron skillet. Add 2 slices to the skillet and cook for about 3 minutes per side, until lightly browned and slightly toasted. Repeat with the remaining slices, adding about 1 tablespoon bacon grease per batch. Serve warm, topped with Caramel-Pecan Syrup.

TIP

Make the Cream of Wheat the night before and chill overnight for a quicker breakfast.

Caramel-Pecan Syrup

PREP TIME: 5 minutes
TOTAL TIME: 15 minutes
MAKES ABOUT 1½ CUPS

1 stick butter

½ cup light corn syrup

½ cup heavy cream

2 tablespoons light brown sugar

2 tablespoons granulated sugar

1 teaspoon vanilla extract

2 tablespoons whiskey (optional)

1 cup chopped pecans

1. Melt the butter in a small saucepan over low heat. Whisk in the corn syrup, cream, brown sugar, and granulated sugar until smooth.

2. Increase the heat to medium and whisk in the vanilla, whiskey (if using), and pecans.

3. Bring to a boil, stirring constantly. Continue to boil for 4 minutes, or until the mixture thickens to a syrup. Serve warm over the fried Cream of Wheat slices.

Champing at the Bit

Appetizers and Snacks

Have you heard the old saying, "If babies are crying and kids are restless in church, then the fish are biting?"

It was always hard for me, my two older brothers, and my sister to stay still for long during church. In fact, I think our limit was about forty-five minutes. Well, one Sunday, I remember the preacher was pushing an hour-long sermon. You could see folks start to wriggle in their seats. I'm pretty sure inner prayers went from, "Please, Lord, let it rain," to "Please, Lord, I sure hope that roast I've got cooking isn't burning!"

Just when I thought the preacher was going to wrap it up, he gave the signal to the choir to go right into "Shall We Gather at the River?" My head sank into my hands, and I thought to myself, Why can't we just gather at the table? My stomach thinks my throat has been cut!

I tapped Mama on the knee and said, "I'm starving, when is he going to finish?"

"It won't be long," she answered.

After four very long and drawn-out verses, the preacher took a deep breath and I just knew he was going to give the final "Amen."

"Let's all sing 'Precious Lord, Take My Hand,'" he proclaimed.

"Lord," I whispered, "if you are listening, would you take that preacher's hand and lead him to the door—it's dinner time!" Finally, after a few more verses, he finished the service, and I have never seen pews empty so fast. It was like Moses and the Exodus!

We made it to the car, and my brothers and I all got to digging around for our secret hiding places for snacks. It was for serious circumstances just like this that we had hidden away provisions—it was every man for himself! I found some stale crackers in between the seats, but luckily I remembered the homemade jerky we had stashed in the console, and I was relieved to know at least we'd make it back to the house before the starvation kicked in.

As we got closer to home, Mama said, "Y'all act like you're starving worse than some old horse champing at the bit. I hope y'all understood what that preacher said this morning, 'Blessed are those who hunger and thirst for righteousness, for they will be filled.'"

I did know that verse came from Matthew, and I really think that Matthew would have understood our small lack of attention during the service due to grumbling stomachs. So when the horses are champing and the fish are biting, it's time to break out the snacks and appetizers!

———◉◦◉———

———◉◦◉———

Deviled Eggs and Ham

PREP TIME: **25 minutes**

TOTAL TIME: **1 hour and 25 minutes**

MAKES 12 DEVILED EGGS

6 large eggs

1 (2.25-ounce) can deviled ham

2 tablespoons mayonnaise

2 tablespoons sweet relish

3 to 4 teaspoons Dijon mustard

Salt and black pepper

Smoked paprika and chopped green onions for topping

Deviled eggs have been around a long time, but Shannon has taken this traditional dish to an even more devilish level by adding deviled ham. The mashed yolks are also blended with sweet relish and Dijon mustard, for a tang that goes well with the ham.

———— ◆•◆ ————

1. In a medium saucepan, bring water to a boil. Add the eggs and boil for 10 minutes. Remove the eggs from the water and place in ice water to cool. Gently crack and peel off the shells, then cut the eggs in half lengthwise.

2. Spoon out the yolks into a small bowl. Add the deviled ham and mash with a fork until smooth.

3. Mix in the mayonnaise, relish, mustard, and salt and pepper to taste. Sample the mixture and adjust the mayo, relish, and mustard to your taste.

4. Spoon the yolk mixture into the egg whites. Cover and refrigerate for about 1 hour, until chilled.

5. Sprinkle with smoked paprika and green onions before serving.

TIP

For a fancier presentation, place the yolk mixture in a small plastic sandwich bag and snip off one corner to make a piping bag. Squeeze the mixture into the egg whites.

Cowboy Guacamole

PREP TIME: **10 minutes**
TOTAL TIME: **10 minutes**
MAKES 2 TO 3 CUPS

4 large avocados, halved and pitted

1 small white onion, finely chopped

1 Roma tomato, seeded and finely chopped

1 large garlic clove, minced

1 to 2 tablespoons diced pickled jalapeños, plus some juice

Salt and black pepper

Garlic powder (optional)

Tortilla chips for serving

For a crowd-pleasing appetizer, what's better than a good guacamole? There are a few tricks to making it. First, use a potato masher and always leave some texture. Second, use a white onion for a slightly sweet and clean flavor. Third, use pickled jalapeños instead of fresh. I also like to stir in a little of the jalapeño juice for more kick.

1. In a medium bowl, mash the avocados with a potato masher. Be sure not to mash until completely smooth—you want some texture.

2. Stir in half the onion and adjust to taste. Stir in the tomato, garlic, jalapeños, and salt and pepper to taste. I also like to start by adding ½ tablespoon of the jalapeño juice, then I adjust any of the ingredients as needed. For more garlic flavor, you can also sprinkle in a little garlic powder.

3. Serve at room temperature or chilled, with tortilla chips.

B Honey's Bruschetta

PREP TIME: **15 minutes**
TOTAL TIME: **45 minutes**
MAKES ABOUT 2 CUPS

1½ cups chopped seeded tomatoes

¼ cup finely chopped fresh basil

½ teaspoon salt

1½ teaspoons minced garlic

1 tablespoon extra-virgin olive oil

½ to 1 cup crumbled feta cheese

Crackers or toasted baguette slices for serving

This recipe comes courtesy of my sweet sister-in-law Bridget, or B Honey, as she's known in the family. This is her go-to party appetizer and it's always a hit, especially in the summer, when fresh 'maters are picked straight from the vine. There isn't a lot to it, which is why I like it too. Chopped tomatoes are blended with fresh basil, garlic, and a little olive oil. Toss in some feta cheese for a sweet tang and serve up on toasted baguette slices for a crunch. This is also good on grilled chicken.

1. Drain the tomatoes well to remove excess moisture, then combine them with the basil, salt, and garlic in a medium bowl. Stir in the olive oil.

2. Stir in ½ cup of the feta cheese to start. The cheese will help absorb some of the moisture. You want the mixture to have a little juice but not be too soupy. Add more cheese as needed.

3. Cover and set aside at room temperature for 30 minutes before serving. Serve with crackers or on toasted baguette slices.

There are three things you're born into this life with: God, family, and your word. Be careful not to tarnish any of them.

The Farrier and the Barber

Haircuts were pretty basic when I was growing up—just a simple buzz. It did save on shampoo and towels, and there sure wasn't a need for a comb. But there is one particular haircut that I've tried to forget, and it all started the day before I was supposed to begin second grade.

We were all gathered around the supper table the night before when Mama said to Pa, "Them boys need a haircut before school starts." Back then, town-bought haircuts cost a dollar apiece, and when you multiply that by three, well, that is three whole dollars that could be spent on groceries or other, more important things.

My dad was a farrier (horseshoer) on the side, and that particular day he had put more shoes on than a woman at a "buy one, get one free" sale at Sears, Roebuck. He was plumb tired by supper, and the suggestion of being a barber was a surprise to him.

"One of y'all go to the barn and get the horse clippers, get a stool, and let's go to the porch," he said. Did he say horse clippers? We had never had a haircut with them before; he generally used a small pair of scissors from under the sink. Pa's reasoning for the big ones was he would be done in half the time, and besides, he just had the blades sharpened.

Randy was the oldest, so he got to sit on the stool first. He looked like a feller being led to the gallows. Pa kept a steady hand on the clippers and his other massive hand holding on to Randy's shoulder. It was over in the blink of an eye, and Randy ran for the barn like a chicken, wobbling and hollering.

Dale was next on the stool. I heard Pa say, "You better sit still, or this is going to hurt!" When Dale came around the corner of the house, he looked a little dazed and his head was slightly notched. I ran in the house and begged Mama to let me go to school without a haircut, but she insisted and told Pa to be easy on me because my head wasn't very big.

"Sit down, Tudor [his nickname for me], and let's get this over with; I'm getting tired of holding these things up," Pa muttered. When he turned that device back on, the clank of metal thrashing against metal sounded like someone had put a toaster in the washing machine. The smell was like when we branded yearlings. "Best be still," Pa warned, "or I'm going to gouge your hide or maybe even an ear."

After several licks to my head, I cried out, and Mama came running. I could tell by her look that something was wrong. Pa blamed me for squirming. "I can't believe you would do that to him!" Mama said.

"Aw, it don't look too bad, and besides, it's just school, it ain't a beauty contest," he replied.

When I came around the house, Dale and Randy were both laughing. I rubbed my head, and it felt lumpy and sore. I ran in the house to the bathroom and looked in the mirror. Surely Mama wouldn't let me go to school looking like this. Who would be laughing in the morning when Dale and Randy had to go to school and I got to stay home eating ice cream until my hair grew back? Unfortunately, the next morning, we were all loaded into the car headed for school.

I got some looks, laughs, and pointing fingers. Finally the teacher called me up to her desk and said, "You better come with me." She escorted me to the principal's office, and as she headed into the principal's office a few minutes later, she handed me a note. "Go home and give this to your mother," she said.

All right! I thought. I'm going to get out of school after all!

Mama was hanging clothes out on the line when I walked up and handed her the note. As she began to read it I heard her scream my name—and I mean all *three* names: "Rodney Kent Rollins, you get in that car right now; we're taking you back to school!"

When we pulled up to the school, Mama yanked me up to the office and told me to sit down and be quiet; she was going to handle it.

When she came out of the principal's office, she looked at me and said, "I will see you after school," and she walked out.

The principal escorted me back to my classroom and told me, "I'm sure sorry, son, about the mix-up."

When Pa came home later that night, Mama lit into him like a hen protecting her chick from a cat. She threw that letter at him and said, "Read this and tell me then how proud you are of your handiwork."

Dear Mrs. Rollins,

It is with our best interest and the interest of the other students and their safety that we take this action. We cannot tolerate or overlook this type of exposure to the other students in the school system, as well as the staff here at Sallie Gillentine Elementary School. That is why we feel we should take this action now instead of after school to prevent the spread and possibly an outbreak of your child's condition. We have made the conclusion that your son, Rodney Kent, has RINGWORMS and should be isolated from the other students until this matter has been resolved.

Sincerely,
Sam Crow
Grade School Principal

Pa just looked at it and said, "They ain't got a clue—them ain't ringworms, those are clipper burns. Those folks we got teaching down there ain't got no common sense at all." At that point, Mama told us kids to go outside and play.

To this day, I never knew what she told Pa, but one thing I know for sure is it was town-bought haircuts from then on. I guess if I learned anything from this, it is to never ask a farrier to do a barber's job.

Paniolo Pineapple-Pepper Poppers

PREP TIME: **15 minutes**
TOTAL TIME: **35 minutes**
MAKES 20 TO 24 POPPERS

8 slices thick-cut bacon

1 (8-ounce) package cream cheese, softened

1 (15.25-ounce) can pineapple chunks, drained well

1 cup shredded cheddar cheese

10 to 12 large assorted sweet mini peppers or jalapeños, stems removed

Store-bought barbecue sauce for brushing

TIP

Mini peppers come in red, orange, and yellow. They can vary greatly in size, so you may have leftover cream cheese mixture.

Paniolo is the Hawaiian word for a cowboy, and this recipe gives an island twist to baked pepper poppers by stuffing them with cream cheese mixed with pineapple chunks. It's an appropriate homage to our island cowhands. Sweet mini peppers will give a change of flavor from the usual jalapeños.

———◆◆———

1. Preheat the oven to 400°F.

2. Place the bacon on a baking sheet and bake, without turning, for about 10 minutes, until it is about half to three-quarters done. Drain the bacon on a paper towel or wire rack until cool enough to handle, then cut each slice into thirds. Wipe off the baking sheet. Leave the oven on.

3. Meanwhile, whisk the cream cheese in a medium bowl until smooth. Chop the pineapple and mix it in, then mix in the cheddar cheese.

4. Cut the peppers in half lengthwise and remove any veins and seeds.

5. Spoon the cream cheese mixture into the pepper halves. Lay a piece of bacon on top of each one and push it down slightly onto the cheese. Generously brush the bacon with barbecue sauce.

6. Place the stuffed peppers on the baking sheet and bake for 15 to 20 minutes, until the bacon is crispy and the peppers soften slightly. Serve hot.

Doubt and fear can't ride with you, if you first saddle up with faith.

East-Meets-West Refried Bean Roll-Up

PREP TIME: **15 minutes**

TOTAL TIME: **25 minutes**

MAKES 10 TO 12 ROLL-UPS

1 (16-ounce) can refried beans (or about 2 cups Ranch Refried Beans, page 143)

¼ cup sour cream

1 (4-ounce) can chopped green chiles

½ cup finely chopped yellow onion

1 (1-pound) package egg roll wrappers

¾ to 1½ cups shredded pepper jack cheese

Peanut or canola oil for frying

Traditional Southwestern flavors of refried beans meet up with an Asian-inspired egg roll. The beans are mixed with green chiles and onion, topped with pepper jack cheese, wrapped up in an egg roll wrapper, and deep-fried for a crunchy bite.

———◆◆◆———

1. In a medium bowl, mix together the refried beans, sour cream, green chiles, and onion.

2. Place an egg roll wrapper on the table, one corner facing you, like a diamond. Spoon about 2 heaping tablespoons of the bean mixture onto the middle of the wrapper. Sprinkle with 1 to 2 tablespoons of the cheese.

3. Fold the right wing of the wrapper toward the middle, followed by the left, so they slightly overlap in the middle. Fold the bottom flap up toward the middle. Dip your finger in a little water to wet the top edge flap, then roll up toward the top and seal. Be sure that the egg roll is sealed all the way around. Repeat with the remaining beans and cheese. (You won't use all the wrappers in the package.)

4. In a large saucepan or Dutch oven, heat 3 to 4 inches of oil to 350°F. Add the egg rolls to the oil a few at a time and deep-fry, turning occasionally, until golden brown, 2 to 3 minutes. Let cool slightly on a paper towel or wire rack. Serve hot.

Shrimp Ceviche

PREP TIME: 25 minutes

TOTAL TIME: 4 hours and
25 minutes

MAKES ABOUT 6 CUPS

1 pound uncooked small
shrimp, peeled and deveined

2 tomatoes, chopped

½ cup finely chopped
purple onion

1 large jalapeño, finely
chopped

½ cucumber, peeled and
finely chopped

2 garlic cloves, minced

5 bay leaves, crumbled

Juice of 4 large limes

Juice of ½ lemon

1 teaspoon chili powder

1 teaspoon salt

½ teaspoon ground oregano

½ teaspoon garlic powder

½ teaspoon black pepper

1 avocado (semifirm), chopped

Tortilla chips or crackers
for serving

No cooking required for this cool, crisp marinated seafood salsa, with chunks of avocado, tomato, cucumber, and jalapeño for a little bite. It's a perfect summer starter. Unlike traditional ceviche recipes, this one calls for cooked shrimp and marinates in a bold blend of Mexican spices.

1. In a large saucepan, cover the shrimp with water. Bring to a boil over high heat for 1 to 3 minutes, until the shrimp turn pink. Drain and let cool in ice water. Cut each shrimp in half.

2. Place the shrimp in a large bowl. Stir in the tomatoes, onion, jalapeño, cucumber, garlic, and bay leaves. Stir in the lime juice and lemon juice until well combined.

3. In a small bowl, whisk together the chili powder, salt, oregano, garlic powder, and pepper.

4. Slowly add the seasonings to the shrimp mixture, stirring to combine. Cover and refrigerate for at least 4 hours, or until ready to serve. The longer it sits, the better the flavor. Stir in the chopped avocado just before serving with tortilla chips or crackers.

TIP

Roll the limes and lemons around against a hard surface using the palm of your hand before cutting. This will help release more juice.

Let your light shine before others,
that they may see your good deeds
and glorify your Father in heaven.

— Matthew 5:16

Honey-Horseradish Chicken Wings

PREP TIME: **1 hour and 15 minutes**
TOTAL TIME: **2 hours**
MAKES ABOUT 6 SERVINGS

½ cup ketchup

¼ cup honey

3 tablespoons prepared horseradish

2 teaspoons lemon juice

2 teaspoons balsamic vinegar

2½ pounds chicken wings

Coarsely ground black pepper

Whether it's game day or you just need to step up your game in the wings department, give this recipe a shot. The zing of the horseradish balances the honey's sweetness.

1. In a small bowl, whisk together the ketchup, honey, horseradish, lemon juice, and vinegar.

2. Place the chicken wings in a large bowl or zippertop bag. Reserve about ½ cup of the sauce, add the rest to the chicken, and toss to coat well. Cover and refrigerate for 1 hour. Remove from the refrigerator about 20 minutes before cooking.

3. Preheat the oven to 400°F. Set a wire rack on a baking sheet.

4. Arrange the wings in a single layer on the rack. Baste with the reserved sauce and sprinkle with black pepper. Cook for 40 to 45 minutes, turning halfway through and basting again with the reserved sauce. The wings are done when the juices run clear. Sprinkle with more black pepper and serve hot or warm.

Crispy Bacon–Cheesy Steak Fries

PREP TIME: **4 hours and 20 minutes**

TOTAL TIME: **4 hours and 35 minutes**

MAKES 8 TO 10 SERVINGS

2 (12-ounce) steaks (New York strip, rib eye, sirloin)

Lime juice

Salt and black pepper

Peanut or canola oil

1 (20-ounce) bag crinkle-cut French fries

1 pound bacon, cooked and cut into 2-inch pieces

2 cups shredded mozzarella cheese

2 cups shredded cheddar cheese

2 cups shredded pepper jack cheese

1 medium yellow onion, chopped

2 jalapeños, finely chopped

If you're a fan of loaded nachos, we've got a new take on them. We start with crinkle-cut fries, because they hold the ingredients better. Top those with generous helpings of tender steak, bacon, onions, jalapeños, and 6 whopping cups of shredded cheese. I told you these were cheesy! The original recipe was done all on the grill, so don't be afraid to take this dish to the backyard.

1. Rub the steaks with lime juice and season both sides with salt and pepper to taste. Cover and refrigerate for at least 4 hours. Remove from the fridge 20 to 30 minutes before cooking.

2. Preheat the oven to 350°F.

3. Heat a large cast-iron skillet over medium-high heat. Lightly oil the skillet, add the steaks, and cook for 3 to 4 minutes per side, or until medium rare. Remove and cut into bite-sized pieces. Set aside in a warm place.

4. In a large saucepan or Dutch oven, heat 3 to 4 inches of oil to 350°F. Add the taters and deep-fry until golden brown and crispy, stirring occasionally. Remove with a slotted spatula and drain on a paper towel or wire rack.

5. Spread half the fries on a large rimmed baking sheet, followed by a layer of half the bacon, cheeses, onion, jalapeños, and steak. Repeat the layers.

6. Bake for 10 to 15 minutes, until all the cheese has melted. Serve.

Okie to English

A Northerner's Guide to Southern Slang

I'm an honorary Okie. I grew up in Nevada, and only moved to the Great Plains about nine years ago. While I never considered myself a Northerner, I quickly learned from the people down in this neck of the woods that practically anywhere above Kansas is considered the North.

My first experience with an Oklahoman was when I talked to Kent over the phone. He was coming to my hometown to host a cooking workshop and do some storytelling and I was helping coordinate the event. I couldn't understand a word he was saying. When I get uncomfortable, I laugh, so as the conversation progressed, I began laughing more and more. After we hung up, Kent thought he was hilarious, and I thought I needed a translator.

But after a few years of being married to this Okie, my ear has become fine-tuned to the language. So as a service to the other Northerners out there, I've compiled a list of Southern sayings and their translations.

—Shannon

It's coming a frog strangler!	There is a storm coming with possible flooding.
Skirt alert—better put a rock in your pocket.	High winds are present: You better be mindful of your skirt and don't blow away.
Colder than a well digger's butt in a forty-foot hole.	Temperatures are frigid, reaching freezing.
Finer than frog's hair.	I'm doing well, thank you for asking.
He's tighter than bark on a tree.	That gentleman is extremely frugal.
His elevator don't go to the top floor.	That gentleman is lacking in common sense.
I don't know if I should scratch my watch or wind my butt.	I am very confused.
Takes a big dog to weigh a ton.	It's not possible to do in this current situation.
I'm hungrier than a one-winged chicken hawk!	I haven't had a thing to eat all day and I'm famished!
Worse than being a long-tailed cat in a room full of rocking chairs.	I'm very nervous about this situation.

Easy No-Dehydrator Jerky

PREP TIME: **6 hours and 45 minutes**

TOTAL TIME: **9 hours and 45 minutes**

MAKES **5 TO 6 SERVINGS**

2 pounds beef chuck roast, bottom round, or brisket

¼ cup soy sauce

2½ tablespoons liquid smoke

2 tablespoons Worcestershire sauce

2 tablespoons light brown sugar

2 teaspoons salt

1 teaspoon unseasoned meat tenderizer

1 teaspoon onion powder

1 teaspoon smoked paprika

1 teaspoon garlic powder

½ teaspoon coarsely ground black pepper

Jerky is the road warrior's survival snack. You'll find it at every convenience store, but the price will nearly bankrupt a person, and it doesn't pack as much flavor as our version. The marinade is an old family recipe that includes liquid smoke and smoked paprika to give a fire-kissed flavor. For tang, we've mixed in soy sauce and Worcestershire, and it's all balanced with a little brown sugar for sweetness. You don't have a dehydrator? Not to worry, because we're sharing a trick to turn your conventional oven into one.

———◆◆◆———

1. Freeze the meat for about 40 minutes, just until firm, so it can be thinly sliced easier.

2. Meanwhile, whisk together the remaining ingredients in a large bowl.

3. Remove the meat from the freezer and cut into thin slices. Cut off any excess fat around the edges; this will prevent spoilage and allow for faster curing.

4. Add the meat to the bowl with the sauce and toss to coat well. Cover and refrigerate for 6 hours or overnight. The longer the meat sits, the better the flavor.

5. Remove two racks from the oven and cover them with foil. Preheat the oven to 180°F.

6. Arrange the meat strips on the foiled racks, making sure they lie flat and are not touching each other. Place the racks in the oven.

7. Close the oven door and wedge a towel or pot holder in between the door and the oven, just enough to create a small

opening for airflow. (This will allow moisture to release while the meat is cooking.)

8. About 1½ hours in, flip the meat over and rotate the racks. Continue cooking for another 1½ hours, or until the jerky is dry. You can cook the jerky longer if you want a crunchier texture.

9. Remove the racks from the oven and let the jerky cool on a wire rack until dried. The jerky can be stored on a paper towel in a zippertop bag for up to 5 days, or it can be frozen for up to 6 months.

Scotch Eggs

PREP TIME: **25 minutes**
TOTAL TIME: **35 minutes**
MAKES 6 SERVINGS

7 large eggs

2½ cups panko bread crumbs

2 teaspoons black pepper

1 teaspoon dry mustard

1 teaspoon paprika or smoked paprika

1 teaspoon salt

1 tablespoon water

1 pound ground breakfast sausage

¾ cup finely chopped green onions

Peanut or canola oil for frying

Yellow mustard or a mix of mustard and prepared horseradish for serving

Now, some of you saw this recipe and immediately thought, "All right, I love a stiff drink with my eggs!" Not so fast: While these little fellers are a pub classic, there's actually no Scotch involved. A soft-boiled egg is wrapped in seasoned sausage and then generously coated in panko bread crumbs and deep-fried. And yes, you can also serve these for breakfast. Be sure not to overboil the eggs, because you will cook them again when you fry them.

---

1. In a medium saucepan, bring water to a boil. Add 6 of the eggs and boil for 6½ to 7 minutes for a soft boil. Transfer the eggs to ice water to cool. Carefully remove the eggshells and pat the eggs dry with a paper towel.

2. Meanwhile, in a small bowl, combine the bread crumbs, pepper, mustard, paprika, and salt. In another small bowl, whisk the remaining egg with the water.

3. In a medium bowl, mix the sausage and green onions well with your hands. Pinch off the sausage into 6 equal pieces. Place each sausage piece between sheets of waxed paper and roll out to a very thin circle. Rolling the sausage out thinly will ensure the meat cooks through entirely when frying.

4. Place an egg in the middle of a sausage circle and form the sausage around the egg. Press firmly and remove any excess sausage, if needed. Repeat with the remaining eggs and sausage. You can dip your hands in cold water to help keep the sausage from sticking to your hands while forming.

5. Brush a sausage ball with the egg wash, then roll in the bread crumbs to generously coat, pressing them into the sausage gently. Repeat with the remaining sausage balls.

6. In a large saucepan or Dutch oven, heat 3 to 4 inches of oil to 350°F. Place the sausage balls in the oil and deep-fry, rolling them occasionally, for 4 to 5 minutes, until they are a deep golden brown. Cool slightly on a wire rack or paper towel. Serve with mustard or mustard-horseradish.

A Helping Hand and Second Helpings

Salads, Soups, and Breads

In the spring and fall months, branding and working season for cattle is accompanied by a ritual called neighboring up. Neighbors from around the county come together to help one another out with the chores. No money ever changes hands, but we all know that the next weekend we'll all be over at someone else's place to help out in the same way.

I was about fifteen when we were helping a couple on a hot and muggy day in May, and there were 150 head of calves that needed to be worked. When we were about half through, I remember overhearing one of the old fellers say, "We better get paid well today, I'm working up a powerful strong appetite!" I thought to myself, *Wow, we are actually going to get cash money this time!*

I made my way around the branding pen to where my older brother was. "Hey, Randy," I whispered. "Did you hear we're going to get real spending money for working today?"

He laughed and replied, "We ain't getting no money, but we're going to be paid better than that—with food!"

I looked up and began to see the caravan of cars and pickups roll in along the outside of the old wooden corral. All the ranch wives began unloading the goods. Some set up sawhorses and old plywood to make tables, while others carried the covered dishes they'd made for the coming feast.

Soon the smell of the branding fire faded and the air filled with the aroma of homemade bread. These weren't just any dishes, these were the best of the best. Each wife had a specialty and was known around the county for it. They took great pride in feeding a crew, because it wasn't just about the food, it was about feeding folks in fellowship too.

In the hot spring months, I remember the cool salads that were dished out. They were just what we needed after working a dusty set of pens. And in the fall, large pots of warm soups would line the makeshift tables. This was a pasture potluck at its finest, and I often went back for a second helping . . . or even a third.

This was the best kind of payment I could have ever received. As I looked around at folks holding a full plate in their lap and heard their laughter filling the air, it occurred to me that no amount of money could buy a moment like this. This wasn't just about doing a job, it was about supporting one another. It didn't matter if we worked two or two hundred cows, we all took pride in helping each other.

You have two hands that are meant to serve. Whether it's serving food or each other—just make sure you serve up enough.

———————◦◦———————

———————◦◦———————

Cheesy Tater Soup

PREP TIME: **15 minutes**
TOTAL TIME: **25 minutes**
MAKES 6 TO 8 SERVINGS

6 large russet potatoes

1 large yellow onion, chopped

1 stick butter, cut into tablespoons

5 cups milk

2 teaspoons garlic powder

Salt and black pepper

1 pound Velveeta cheese, cubed

Nothing says comfort food like a good tater soup, but what makes it even more of a comfort classic is cheese . . . and lots of it! I like to use Velveeta on the chuck wagon, because it's easy to pack and doesn't need refrigeration; it also melts down easily and gives the soup a rich and creamy flavor. This soup is loaded with russet taters and a little garlic powder, but you can use it as a base and add in anything else you'd like, including sausage and broccoli.

1. Peel and cut the potatoes into small chunks. In a large pot, cover the potatoes with cold water and bring to a boil over high heat. Boil for about 5 minutes, then stir in the onion. Continue to boil just until the potatoes are slightly tender, about 3 minutes. Be careful not to overboil the potatoes, or they'll turn mushy.

2. Drain the water from the potatoes. Stir in the butter, milk, garlic powder, and salt and pepper to taste. Bring back to a boil.

3. Reduce the heat to a simmer, stir in the Velveeta, and cook, stirring frequently, until melted and smooth, about 10 minutes. Serve.

Buckaroo Cabbage and Thyme Soup

PREP TIME: **15 minutes**

TOTAL TIME: **1 hour**

MAKES 6 TO 8 SERVINGS

1 (32-ounce) carton vegetable
or chicken broth

7 cups water

1 (8- to 10-ounce) ham hock

1 head green cabbage, coarsely
chopped

4 large carrots, peeled and
sliced ¼-inch thick

1 large yellow onion, coarsely
chopped

2 garlic cloves, minced

2 tablespoons minced
fresh thyme

1 tablespoon smoked paprika

Salt and black pepper

Shannon is from northern Nevada, which is Basque country, and they're known for their cabbage soup. She has put her own spin on this recipe with fresh thyme and smoked paprika. The cabbage simmers until tender in the full-bodied broth seasoned with ham hock, for a rich, smoky flavor.

— ◆◆ —

1. Add the broth, water, ham hock, cabbage, and carrots to a large pot. Cover and bring to a boil. Boil for about 10 minutes, stirring occasionally.

2. Stir in the onion, garlic, thyme, and paprika and season with salt and pepper to taste. Reduce the heat to a simmer and cook, stirring occasionally, for 30 to 45 minutes, until the vegetables are tender. Season again, if needed, and serve. If storing, remove the ham hock and discard. Refrigerate for up to 3 to 4 days.

TIP

If you don't have a ham hock, you can substitute about 7 slices uncooked thick-cut bacon, chopped.

My dad said there ain't no such thing as luck. You just hang on tighter or get bucked off.

A Second Opinion

Many is the day that I have spent
Hauling hay and fixing fence.

Many is the hour I've spent astraddle,
Bouncing my backside in the seat of a saddle.

And as times have gone by, the chores haven't changed,
But my old body has, and it just don't react the same.

The spills and the falls, well they begin to hurt more,
And each day's work feels like a month's worth of chores.

Has the ground got harder or am I insane?
The things that used to be fun now cause pain.

As I think of the things that really do hurt,
It's the hours in the saddle that seem to be the worst.

Feels like there's a rock in the middle of my seat,
And when my horse trots, it sends a sharp pain down to my feet.

That sharp pain is the one that I most fear,
For when my horse reaches a trot, I almost shed a tear.

I had coped with this problem for quite some time,
And I was ready to find a solution to this agony of mine.

I called the doc and an appointment I made.
I might have been a little embarrassed, but I sure wasn't afraid.

I explained to Doc this little problem of mine.
He said, "Slip into this gown, everything's going to be just fine."

Well, this little gown didn't seem to fit,
And the part left sticking out was the part where I sit.

I laid there on the table with my backside in the air.
I said, "Hang on a minute, Doc—is that necessary, does that part need to be bare?"

"Oh, this problem you've got, it's really nothing to avoid.
It's actually quite simple, it's a thing we call a hemorrhoid."

"A hemorrhoid?! Well, Doc, what might be the cure?"
He said, "Nothing major, but we're going to have to cut it off, that's for sure."

"Cut it off!" I cried in fright.
"Hang on a minute, Doc, I think a second opinion might be right."

He said, "Well, a second opinion, I really don't see the need."
That's when I gathered my hat and boots and left with a sudden burst of speed.

I felt I was lucky to get out of there with my life,
'Cause no doc is going to get near my backside, especially with a knife!

Well, as for this little problem, I ain't got rid of it yet,
But one thing's for certain, I won't go back to that crazy vet!

French Onion Soup

PREP TIME: **1 hour**
TOTAL TIME: **1 hour and 35 minutes**
MAKES **4 TO 6 SERVINGS**

4 large Vidalia onions

1 stick butter

2 garlic cloves, minced

2 (32-ounce) cartons beef broth

⅓ cup white wine

3 bay leaves

1 tablespoon Worcestershire sauce

1 tablespoon beef bouillon powder

1 (5-ounce) bag seasoned croutons

1 to 1½ cups shredded provolone, mozzarella, or Gruyère cheese

Shredded Parmesan cheese for sprinkling

For this simple soup, you just need a little patience. The onions require plenty of time to cook down, and you'll have to use lower heat so they caramelize. The rich, buttery onions are then simmered in a savory beef broth with bay leaves, white wine, and a hint of Worcestershire sauce. This is great to do in a cast-iron skillet, since it will not only build a good seasoning on your pan, but the skillet helps flavor the onions. Traditionally, the soup is topped with a baguette and Gruyère cheese. Gruyère is a little hard to come by in rural Oklahoma, so we top it with seasoned croutons and provolone or mozzarella cheese.

1. Cut the root ends off the onions, then cut the onions in half and thinly slice them.

2. Melt ½ stick of the butter in each of two large cast-iron skillets. Evenly divide the onions between the skillets and cook over medium-low heat, stirring occasionally, for 45 minutes to 1 hour, until the onions are a deep golden color and reduce in size significantly. You don't want them to brown too quickly, so you may have to reduce the heat while cooking.

3. Stir the garlic into one of the skillets and cook for 1 minute more.

4. Add the beef broth, white wine, bay leaves, and Worcestershire sauce to a large pot. Stir in the onions. Bring to a boil, then stir in the beef bouillon and reduce the heat to low. Simmer for about 30 minutes, stirring occasionally.

5. Preheat the broiler.

TIP

Slice the onions evenly to
ensure even cooking, and
watch them carefully, lowering
the heat if necessary so they
don't brown too quickly or burn
at the edges.

6. Remove the bay leaves and ladle the soup into heat-proof bowls. Top each serving with some croutons and 3 to 4 tablespoons of the provolone, then sprinkle with some Parmesan. Broil for a few minutes, or until the cheese is bubbling and lightly browned. Serve immediately.

CAST-IRON CORRAL

NO SOAP! TWO EASY WAYS TO CLEAN CAST IRON

Some folks are intimidated by cast iron, because they don't know how to take care of it. Here are two easy ways to clean your cast. Remember: Never use soap, because it can break down the natural nonstick finish, called seasoning. You want to be careful when scrubbing cast iron so as not to remove that seasoning.

1. Steam Clean

After cooking, remove the pan from the heat and let it cool just slightly. Run water from the tap until it's hot. Carefully rinse the warm cast iron under the hot water. Don't use soap! With a clean sponge, lightly scrub any debris. It should come off easily. Rinse until clean. Dry with a lint-free cloth, reheat to dry out any excess moisture, season the warm cast iron by lightly rubbing with a bit of oil, and then wipe again with the cloth.

2. Scrub with a Potato and Salt

Cut a raw potato in half, preferably a russet (baking) potato. Sprinkle some coarse salt in the bottom of your cast piece. Lightly scrub the salt around the pan with the cut side of the potato until any food is removed. Rinse the pan with warm water. Dry with a cloth, reheat to dry out any excess moisture, season the warm cast iron by lightly rubbing with a bit of oil, and then wipe again with the cloth.

TO PREVENT OR REMOVE STICKINESS

I'm often asked, "Why is my cast iron sticky?" There are two common reasons why cast iron develops buildup on the cooking surface, causing it to feel tacky or gummy.

Using Too Much Oil When Seasoning

Cast iron should be seasoned after every use. More oil is not better. Depending on the size of the skillet or Dutch oven, I typically use about a nickel- to a quarter-sized amount of oil. You just need a very thin layer on the bottom and up the sides. After applying a thin layer of oil, let the cast set a few minutes, then go back and wipe it around with a clean lint-free cloth to absorb any excess oil. If the cast seems to be a little tacky, you can reheat it on the stovetop and wipe again.

Seasoning When Cast Iron Is Cold

Cast iron needs to be warm when seasoned. If the iron is not warm, the oil won't adhere properly. After cleaning your pan, place it on a burner over medium to medium-high heat until it is evenly warmed. Don't heat to a smoking point. Turn the heat off and rub a light layer of oil around with a lint-free cloth.

IF YOUR CAST IRON IS ALREADY STICKY

For mild stickiness, a good washing with hot water and light scrubbing with a sponge should do. For more stubborn stickiness, place the cast iron over high heat and get the piece very hot, which will help release any residue. Wipe clean with a rag. Alternatively, steam clean as directed on page 91.

OUR FAVORITE OILS FOR SEASONING CAST IRON

I recommend seasoning cast iron after every use. Nearly any type of cooking oil can be used. However, there are certain oils that we prefer depending on the situation. We don't recommend using bacon grease, lard, or vegetable oil for seasoning because they can become rancid over time. But if you are using a seasoning method that works for you, by all means keep doing it!

Avocado and **grapeseed oils** are great all-around oils for seasoning because they adhere easily to cast iron. **Flaxseed oil** is great as a seasoning base for the same reason, but over time it can become brittle, so I recommend switching to one of the other oils after initial use.

Olive oil has been our seasoning oil of choice for years. It's cost-effective and performs particularly well as a seasoning for Dutch ovens because it doesn't turn rancid easily.

Collard Green and Black-Eyed Pea Soup

PREP TIME: **25 minutes**

TOTAL TIME: **1 hour**

MAKES ABOUT 6 SERVINGS

1 (32-ounce) carton plus 1 cup chicken broth

2 (15.8-ounce) cans black-eyed peas (undrained) or 2½ to 3 pounds fresh

4 carrots, peeled and thinly sliced

3 roasted green chiles, chopped or 1 (4-ounce) can chopped green chiles

2 garlic cloves, minced

3 tablespoons vegetable oil

1 (1- to 1½-pound) ham steak

1 yellow onion, chopped

1 bunch collard greens (1½ to 2 pounds), stemmed and chopped

2 teaspoons white vinegar

We originally came up with this soup to celebrate the New Year. You see, it's a Southern tradition to have black-eyed peas on New Year's Day for good luck. Folks often add greens too, for wealth. This soup has chunks of ham and black-eyed peas in every bite. When the collards simmer with the spices, their bitterness softens and they take on the flavor of the chicken broth. Serve with some cornbread and you've got a plentiful dish—with some good luck and fortune on the side.

———— •◦• ————

1. Add the chicken broth, black-eyed peas, carrots, green chiles, and garlic to a large saucepan. Bring to a boil, then reduce to a simmer, stirring occasionally.

2. Meanwhile, in a large cast-iron skillet, heat 2 tablespoons of the oil over medium-high heat. Add the ham and lightly brown it, about 2 minutes per side. Remove and chop into bite-sized pieces, then add to the saucepan.

3. Add the onion and 1 tablespoon oil to the skillet and cook over medium heat, stirring occasionally and adding more oil if necessary, until tender, about 5 minutes. Stir in the collard greens, a little bit at a time, and cook for about 5 minutes, stirring occasionally, adding more oil if needed. Stir in the vinegar and cook for another 2 minutes.

4. Scrape the contents of the skillet into the saucepan and cook over medium heat, stirring occasionally, for about 20 minutes. Turn the heat to low and simmer, stirring occasionally, until the carrots are tender, about 15 minutes more. Serve.

Chicken Tortilla Soup

PREP TIME: **30 minutes**

TOTAL TIME: **1 hour**

MAKES ABOUT **6 SERVINGS**

3 boneless, skinless chicken breasts halves

3 garlic cloves, peeled

1 serrano chile

3 teaspoons salt

10 cups water

4 dried guajillo chiles, stemmed, halved, and seeded

2 dried ancho chiles, stemmed, halved, and seeded

1 white onion, halved

3 chiles de árbol, stemmed and seeded (optional)

2 tomatoes, cored and halved

2 (15-ounce) cans black beans

6 flour or corn tortillas

Peanut or canola oil for frying

Queso fresco and sliced avocado for serving

This is a flavorful soup that will sure take the chill off with a variety of traditional Mexican chile peppers. The homemade pepper sauce makes this dish special, and you can usually find these different types of chiles in the international aisle at some grocery stores in plastic bags or online. Fried tortilla strips add a crunch that's great with the warm, spiced soup and cool queso fresco and avocado. You can also get creative and switch up the toppings to suit you.

1. Put the chicken, 1 of the garlic cloves, the serrano chile, and 1 teaspoon of the salt in a large pot. Add the water and bring to a boil, then reduce the heat and simmer for about 25 minutes, until the chicken is tender and cooked through. Remove and discard the serrano and garlic clove.

2. Remove the chicken and set aside to cool; reserve the broth in the pot. When the chicken is cool enough to handle, shred or chop the meat. Set aside.

3. Meanwhile, add the guajillo and ancho chiles, the onion, chiles de árbol (if using for added spice), tomatoes, the remaining 2 garlic cloves, and 1 teaspoon of the salt to a large saucepan and cover with water. Bring to a boil and boil for about 20 minutes, until the chiles are tender.

4. Strain the contents from the pot with a slotted spoon and place them in a blender. Add 1 cup of the water used to cook the chiles (discard the rest) and the remaining 1 teaspoon salt and blend until a smooth sauce forms.

5. Stir the chicken meat back into the pot with the reserved chicken broth. Stir in the black beans and the chile sauce.

(recipe continues)

TIP

For a slightly thicker broth, dissolve 2 tablespoons cornstarch in ¾ cup cold water and stir into the soup with the beans and chile sauce.

Bring back to a boil, then reduce to a simmer and cook for about 30 minutes, to allow the flavors to blend.

6. Meanwhile, cut the tortillas into ½- to ¾-inch-wide strips. In a large saucepan or Dutch oven, heat about 2 inches of oil to 350°F. Add the tortilla strips and fry, stirring frequently, until crispy, 1 to 2 minutes. Remove from the oil with the slotted spoon and drain on a paper towel or wire rack.

7. Ladle the soup into bowls and serve topped with the fried tortilla strips, cheese, and avocado. Serve hot.

Let us be ever mindful of the little blessings in life, especially the ones we take for granted.

Catalina Taco Salad

PREP TIME: **45 minutes**
TOTAL TIME: **50 minutes**
MAKES ABOUT 8 SERVINGS

1 pound ground beef
(80% lean)

1 (1-ounce) package taco
seasoning

¼ cup water

1 head iceberg lettuce,
chopped

1 small yellow onion, chopped

1 heaping cup chopped tomato

1 (15-ounce) can ranch-
style beans or chili beans,
drained well

1 cup shredded cheddar
cheese, plus more for serving

½ to ¾ cup store-bought
Catalina dressing

Nacho Cheese Doritos or corn
chips for serving

*Chopped iceberg lettuce tossed with chunks of tomatoes, sea-
soned ground beef, and chili beans makes a tasty, cool dinner
after a long, hot summer day. Top it off with corn chips—or
our favorite, Nacho Cheese Doritos—and Catalina dressing
for a hearty salad for the crew.*

———◆———

1. Brown the beef in a medium skillet over medium heat,
stirring to break it up. Drain any excess fat.

2. Stir in the taco seasoning and water, reduce the heat to
a simmer, and cook for 10 minutes to allow the flavors to
blend, stirring occasionally.

3. Remove from the heat and let cool slightly, then cover and
cool in the refrigerator for 30 minutes.

4. In a large bowl, toss together the lettuce, onion, and
tomato, then toss in the beef and beans. Top with the cheddar cheese; drizzle with the dressing, to taste.

5. Top the salad with more cheese, lightly break the Doritos
or corn chips and sprinkle them over, and serve.

TIP

If you want to set some of the salad aside for later, add the chips
and dressing at the last minute so the dish stays crispy.

Coleslaw with Tequila-Lime Dressing

PREP TIME: **5 minutes**

TOTAL TIME: **4 hours and 5 minutes**

MAKES ABOUT 6 SERVINGS

1¼ cups mayonnaise

¼ cup honey

Juice of 1 lime

6 tablespoons tequila

1 tablespoon apple cider vinegar

1 (16-ounce) bag tricolor coleslaw

Let's take an old-time backyard barbecue favorite and flavor it up a notch! Instead of just using apple cider vinegar for tang, we also add tequila. Along with the lime juice, it helps break down the cabbage. The enhanced citrus flavor is like a creamy bite of margarita in a cool salad.

————— •••• —————

1. In a small bowl, mix together the mayonnaise, honey, lime juice, tequila, and apple cider vinegar.

2. Pour the coleslaw into a large bowl. Pour the mayonnaise mixture over the coleslaw and mix well. Cover and refrigerate for 4 hours, or until ready to serve. Stir well before serving.

Cool Cucumber-Dill Salad

PREP TIME: **2 hours**
TOTAL TIME: **4 hours**
MAKES 6 TO 8 SERVINGS

2 large cucumbers, peeled and sliced about ⅛-inch thick

½ purple onion, diced

5 tablespoons red wine vinegar

½ cup sour cream

3 tablespoons mayonnaise

1 tablespoon avocado oil or olive oil

1 teaspoon dried dill

Salt and black pepper

Garden fresh just found its way to the table with this light and refreshing salad. We especially like it with something off the grill. The cucumbers and purple onion marinate in red wine vinegar, which has a mellow tang. A creamy mix of sour cream and mayonnaise with a hint of dill smooths everything out.

1. In a large bowl, combine the cucumbers, onion, and red wine vinegar. Cover and refrigerate for 2 hours.

2. In a small bowl, whisk together the sour cream, mayonnaise, oil, and dill.

3. Add the sour cream mixture to the cucumbers and stir well to evenly coat. Season with salt and pepper to taste. Cover and refrigerate for 2 hours, or until ready to serve. Serve cold with a slotted spoon.

Bacon-Artichoke Pasta Salad

PREP TIME: **40 minutes**
TOTAL TIME: **40 minutes**
MAKES ABOUT 6 SERVINGS

⅔ cup mayonnaise

2 tablespoons olive oil

2 teaspoons balsamic vinegar

1 teaspoon apple cider vinegar

1 teaspoon garlic powder

1 teaspoon onion powder

½ teaspoon dried dill

2 tablespoons water

Salt and black pepper

7 slices thick-cut bacon

2 cups bow-tie pasta (uncooked)

2 tablespoons butter, melted

2½ tablespoons grated Parmesan cheese

6 heaping cups chopped romaine lettuce

1 (14-ounce) can artichoke hearts, drained

½ cup shredded Parmesan cheese

TIP

For a quicker preparation, you can substitute 1 cup bacon bits for the bacon.

I don't believe I ever had a salad and a pasta in one dish until Shannon created this—or if I did, it wasn't memorable. This one is. I love the crisp bite of romaine lettuce combined with the softness of the pasta. The bow-tie pasta is coated in butter and grated Parmesan cheese and mixed with chopped artichokes, with thick-cut bacon for a bold flavor. An easy, creamy vinaigrette brings it all together, but you're welcome to pair it with any favorite salad dressing.

———◆◆◆———

1. In a small bowl, whisk together the mayonnaise, olive oil, both vinegars, the garlic powder, onion powder, dill, and water. Season with salt and pepper to taste. Cover and refrigerate the dressing for 30 minutes, or until ready to serve.

2. In a large skillet, cook the bacon over medium-high heat until crispy, 8 to 10 minutes. Let cool on a paper towel or wire rack, then chop.

3. Bring a large pot of salted water to a boil over high heat. Add the pasta and cook until al dente—that's just a fancy word for "firm to the bite." Drain and rinse the pasta under cold water, then drain again well.

4. In a large bowl, toss the pasta with the melted butter, then with the grated Parmesan, until well coated. Add the lettuce and bacon, and toss again. Coarsely chop the artichoke hearts and toss them into the salad.

5. When ready to serve, drizzle the dressing over the salad to taste, and lightly toss to coat. Top with the shredded Parmesan. Season with salt and pepper to taste and serve.

My people will live in peaceful dwelling places,
in secure homes, in undisturbed places of rest.

— Isaiah 32:18

Helen's Layered Cornbread Salad

PREP TIME: **25 minutes**

TOTAL TIME: **1 hour and 30 minutes**

MAKES 6 TO 8 SERVINGS

1 (8.5-ounce) box Jiffy corn muffin mix

1 (4-ounce) can chopped green chiles

1 cup mayonnaise

1 cup sour cream

1 (1-ounce) package ranch dressing mix

1 pound ground beef (80% lean)

4 slices thick-cut bacon, cut into ½-inch pieces

1 (16-ounce) can pinto beans, drained

1 large tomato, chopped

4 green onions, chopped

2 cups shredded cheddar cheese

This recipe comes from our dear friend Helen Isaacs, who has had many years of experience feeding hungry crowds. Helen and her husband, Chris, have twenty-seven grandchildren, so all of her recipes have been well tested! We like this recipe because it's a blend of a taco salad and cornbread. Layers of taco meat, lettuce, cheese, and a creamy ranch-style dressing make for a colorful presentation. This is a great dish to make if you have leftover cornbread.

1. Prepare the corn muffin mix according to the directions on the box. Stir the green chiles into the batter and bake as directed for making cornbread.

2. Meanwhile, in a medium bowl, whisk together the mayonnaise, sour cream, and ranch dressing mix; set aside.

3. In a large skillet, cook the ground beef and bacon together over medium-high heat, stirring to break up the meat, until the beef has browned, about 8 minutes. Drain the grease.

4. When the cornbread has finished baking, let cool to room temperature or refrigerate to speed up the process.

5. Crumble the cornbread with your hands. Spoon half the cornbread into a large bowl. Spread half the ranch dressing mixture on top, followed by half the meat mixture, half the beans, and half the tomatoes, green onions, and cheese. Repeat the layers one more time.

6. Cover and refrigerate for at least 1 hour, or until chilled, before serving.

TIP

If using leftover cornbread, substitute about 4 cups crumbled cornbread for the Jiffy mix and toss in the green chiles.

Mama's Marshmallow-Cranberry Salad

PREP TIME: **6 hours**

TOTAL TIME: **7 hours**

MAKES 8 TO 10 SERVINGS

4 cups fresh cranberries

1¼ cups sugar

1 cup heavy cream

1 (10-ounce) package mini marshmallows

1 (8-ounce) can crushed pineapple, drained

1 cup chopped pecans (optional)

A blend of sweet and tangy, with a little crunch, makes this is our all-time favorite salad or side dish for Thanksgiving and Christmas. Fresh crushed cranberries are mixed with sugar and sit overnight so they soften and sweeten. The next day, they're mixed with whipped cream, pecans, and marshmallows.

———◆———

1. Coarsely grind the cranberries in a food processor. Scrape into a bowl and mix in 1 cup of the sugar. Cover and refrigerate for 6 hours or overnight to allow the cranberries to soften and sweeten.

2. In a large bowl, using an electric mixer, whip the cream with the remaining ¼ cup sugar until stiff. Fold in the cranberries, marshmallows, pineapple, and pecans, if using.

3. Cover and refrigerate for 1 hour, or until chilled. Serve cold.

Don't let what you want get overshadowed by what you already have.

Jalapeño-Cheddar Buttermilk Biscuits

PREP TIME: **1 hour and 25 minutes**
TOTAL TIME: **2 hours and 5 minutes**
MAKES ABOUT 20 BISCUITS

1 (¼-ounce) package
rapid-rise yeast

¾ cup warm water

¼ cup sugar

2 cups buttermilk

½ cup lemon-lime soda
(7 Up, Sprite)

2 tablespoons baking powder

1 teaspoon baking soda

1 teaspoon salt

8 jalapeños, minced

3½ cups shredded cheddar
cheese

4½ to 5 cups all-purpose flour,
plus more for dusting

Y'all have probably guessed that I like my food with a kick. These buttermilk biscuits bake up moist and include some of my favorite ingredients: cheese and jalapeños! But what really makes these unique is the addition of the lemon-lime soda: The carbonation gives the biscuits a light, airy texture. These are a great pairing for any dish.

1. In a large bowl, dissolve the yeast in the warm water. Let rest for about 10 minutes, or until bubbly.

2. Whisk in the sugar, buttermilk, lemon-lime soda, baking powder, baking soda, and salt, then stir in the jalapeños and cheese. Gradually stir in the flour until the dough is soft but not sticky.

3. Turn the dough out onto a floured surface and roll to about ½ inch thick. Cut out about twenty 2½-inch biscuits.

4. Butter the bottom and sides of a 12-inch cast-iron skillet or 9-x-13-inch baking pan. Arrange the biscuits in the skillet or pan so they are touching, then cover and let rise in a warm place for 1 hour, or until doubled in size.

5. Preheat the oven to 375°F with a rack in the middle.

6. Bake for 35 to 40 minutes, or until golden brown. Serve.

Easy Homemade Tortillas

PREP TIME: **20 minutes**
TOTAL TIME: **35 minutes**
MAKES ABOUT TWELVE 8-INCH TORTILLAS

3 cups all-purpose flour, plus more for dusting

2 teaspoons salt

1 teaspoon baking powder

¼ cup shortening or lard (see Tip)

¼ cup bacon grease, cooled

1 cup hot water

This recipe is surprisingly simple and gives you that homemade tortilla flavor. Know what part of the trick is? Bacon grease. Adding a little to the mix really enhances the flavor. Enjoy them in Breakfast Burritos (page 18) or serve with soup.

— • • • —

1. In a large bowl, combine the flour, salt, and baking powder.

2. Cut in the shortening and bacon grease with a spoon until evenly combined and any large chunks of grease/lard are broken up. (The pieces don't need to be as fine as in a pie dough.)

3. Stir in the hot water until combined. With your hands, work the dough into a ball. You can add more hot water, a teaspoon at a time, if needed.

4. Turn the dough out onto a floured surface and knead with your hands for about 2 minutes, adding more flour to take away any stickiness, if needed.

5. Cover the dough and let rest for 10 minutes. (You can refrigerate the dough in a zippertop bag for up to 1 week; bring to room temperature before continuing.)

6. Turn over the dough to lightly flour the outside. Pinch off the dough into 12 pieces roughly the size of a golf ball. Work each piece of dough into a ball, then press down lightly to form rounds roughly the size of your palm. Place the rounds onto the floured surface and roll them out into 8-inch circles.

7. Heat a large cast-iron skillet or griddle over high heat. Shake off any excess flour from a tortilla and place it in the skillet. Cook until it begins to set on one side, 30 seconds to 1½ minutes, patting down any bubbles on the surface (light brown spots may appear depending on the heat of the skillet), then flip and repeat on the other side. Be careful not to overcook the tortilla, or it will become brittle.

8. Repeat with the remaining tortillas, wrapping them in a towel as you go and keeping them warm in a low (200°F) oven until you are ready to serve. Serve warm or at room temperature.

Sweet Hushpuppies, and Savory Ones Too

An old-timer once told me as he was getting ready to fry some fish, "We better do the hushpuppies first so when folks get to hollering, we can serve these and quiet the bark of those hungry hounds!" He was right: Hushpuppies are a great way to transform cornbread into a fried delicacy. Me being from the South, I like mine with a little bite, so I mix the batter up with jalapeño peppers. Shan tells me that people from up North like their cornbread a little sweeter, so she adds some honey and sweet onion to hers, which creates a caramel-like crust. Whichever version you choose, you can't go wrong, 'cause there's crunch in every bite!

1 tablespoon butter

½ cup minced Vidalia onion

1 cup all-purpose flour, plus more for dusting

1 cup yellow cornmeal

¼ cup sugar

2 teaspoons baking powder

1 teaspoon salt

1 large egg

½ cup milk

2 tablespoons honey

Peanut or canola oil for frying

Shannon's Sweet Hushpuppies

1. Melt the butter in a medium skillet over medium heat. Add the onion and cook, stirring occasionally, until tender, about 8 minutes.

2. Meanwhile, in a medium bowl, mix together the flour, cornmeal, sugar, baking powder, and salt.

3. In another medium bowl, whisk together the egg, milk, honey, and onions.

4. Slowly stir the milk mixture into the flour mixture just until combined. Overstirring will cause it to become too moist.

5. Flour your hands and pinch off about two dozen 1-inch balls of the hushpuppy mixture. Be sure not to make these too large or they won't cook through evenly.

6. In a large, saucepan or Dutch oven, heat 3 to 4 inches of oil to between 340°F and 350°F. Add several hushpuppies at a time to the oil and deep-fry, turning frequently, until all sides are a deep golden brown, 3 to 4 minutes. Repeat with the remaining hushpuppies.

7. Remove from the oil with a slotted spoon and let cool slightly on a paper towel or wire rack. Serve hot or at room temperature.

(recipe continues)

PREP TIME: 10 minutes

TOTAL TIME: 20 minutes

MAKES 15 TO 17 HUSHPUPPIES

Kent's Savory Hushpuppies

1 cup yellow cornmeal

¼ cup all-purpose flour,
plus more if needed

1½ teaspoons baking powder

½ teaspoon salt

1 large egg, beaten

¾ cup milk

1 small yellow onion, finely
chopped

4 sweet mini peppers, finely
chopped

2 jalapeños, finely chopped

Peanut or canola oil for frying

1. In a large bowl, combine the cornmeal, flour, baking powder, and salt. Whisk in the egg and milk. Stir in the onion, sweet mini peppers, and jalapeños.

2. With floured hands, form the dough into a ball. Add more flour to the dough to take away excess stickiness, if needed. Pinch off 15 to 17 pieces of the dough and form them into about 2½-x-½-inch cylinders.

3. In a large, saucepan or Dutch oven, heat 3 to 4 inches of oil to 350°F. Drop several of the hushpuppies into the oil at a time and deep-fry, turning frequently, for about 2 to 3 minutes, until light golden brown. Repeat with the remaining hushpuppies.

4. Remove from the oil with a slotted spoon and let cool slightly on a paper towel or wire rack. Serve hot or at room temperature.

Braided Onion French Bread

PREP TIME: **1 hour and 50 minutes**
TOTAL TIME: **2 hours and 20 minutes**
MAKES ONE 15-INCH LOAF

1 teaspoon poppy seeds

1 teaspoon dried minced garlic

1 teaspoon dried onion

2 cups warm water

1 (¼-ounce) package rapid-rise yeast

2 tablespoons sugar

1 tablespoon olive oil

¼ heaping cup minced yellow onion

2 teaspoons salt

3⅓ cups all-purpose flour, plus more if needed

1 large egg white

1 tablespoon water

I have done a lot of braiding in my lifetime, from rawhide to rope, but I had never eaten anything braided until Shan made this recipe. It starts like a classic French bread, but then she adds minced onion to the dough for more flavor. Before baking, she brushes it with an egg wash and sprinkles it with a generous mix of poppy seeds, garlic, and onion to give it that everything-bagel taste. You don't have to braid this recipe—you can just serve it plain as a loaf—but the braiding sure makes for a great presentation. This makes one loaf, but it can easily be doubled, which is what we often do. It makes a good sandwich bread too.

---

1. In a small bowl, combine the poppy seeds, dried garlic, and dried onion.

2. In a large bowl, whisk together the warm water, yeast, and sugar. Let sit for 10 minutes, or until the mixture begins to froth. Mix in the olive oil, fresh onion, and salt. Slowly stir in the flour until combined.

3. Turn the dough out onto a floured surface and knead for 2 to 3 minutes, adding more flour to remove any stickiness, if needed.

4. Butter a large bowl, add the dough, cover, and let sit in a warm place until nearly doubled in size, about 1 hour.

5. Turn the dough out onto a floured surface and turn it over a few times to lightly coat the outside with flour. Cut into 3 equal pieces. Roll each piece into a strand 18 to 20 inches long. Place the strands on the baking sheet and braid them together. Pinch and turn each end under.

TIP

This can also be made in a 10- to 12-inch Dutch oven or cast-iron skillet by wrapping the dough around in a circle for a unique presentation.

6. Cover the loaf with a towel and let sit in a warm place until slightly risen, about 40 minutes.

7. Preheat the oven to 375°F. Butter a baking sheet.

8. In a small bowl, whisk together the egg white and 1 table-spoon water. Lightly brush the top of the loaf with the egg wash, then sprinkle with the poppy seed mixture.

9. Bake for 20 to 30 minutes, until the top and bottom are a light golden brown and the bread sounds hollow when tapped. Cool on a rack. Serve warm or at room temperature.

Pretzel Rolls

PREP TIME: **1 hour and 15 minutes**
TOTAL TIME: **1 hour and 25 minutes**
MAKES 8 ROLLS

1 (¼-ounce) package
rapid-rise yeast

1 tablespoon sugar

1 cup warm water

2 tablespoons vegetable oil

1 teaspoon salt

2¼ cups all-purpose flour,
plus more if needed

6 cups plus 1 tablespoon water

⅓ cup baking soda

1 large egg yolk

Coarse sea salt

I just love a good warm pretzel, and these little fellers have all the classic pretzel pluses—a chewy center and salty pretzel-dough flavor. They are formed into a pretzel shape, and as they bake, they rise to look like a twisted roll. The trick to getting that chewy texture is to boil them in baking soda water first and finish them off in the oven sprinkled with coarse sea salt.

━━━━●━━●━━━

1. In a large bowl, dissolve the yeast and sugar in the warm water. Let sit for 10 minutes, or until it begins to froth.

2. Stir in the oil and salt. Stir in 1 cup of the flour until combined, then stir in the remaining 1¼ cups flour. With your hands, knead the dough for a few minutes. If it's too sticky, add a little flour while kneading. Cover and let rest in a warm spot for about 45 minutes, until nearly doubled in size.

3. Meanwhile, butter a baking sheet and preheat the oven to 425°F with a rack in the middle.

4. Turn the dough out onto a lightly floured surface. Gently punch the dough and divide into 8 pieces. Roll 1 piece out into a long, thin rope. Hold the rope to form a U shape. Cross the two ends over each other, then fold the twisted ends down to the bottom of the U and press to seal. Repeat with the remaining dough.

5. Bring the 6 cups water and the baking soda to a low boil in a large pot. Add a few of the pretzel rolls at a time and boil for about 15 seconds on each side. Remove with a slotted spoon and drain well on paper towels. Place on the baking sheet.

6. In a small bowl, whisk together the egg yolk and 1 tablespoon water. Brush over the rolls and sprinkle with sea salt. Bake for about 10 minutes, or until golden brown.

TIP

If the water begins frothing heavily while you're boiling the pretzels, reduce the heat slightly.

Ride-Alongs

Vegetables and Side Dishes

Everything in life is better with someone special by your side. When I was about eight years old, I overheard my dad telling a bunch of cowboys in the branding pen the news of a big cattle gathering. They were planning on moving a herd about ten miles, and to a young boy, this was the stuff dreams were made of. The plan was to meet at our house the next day at first light, saddle the horses, and ride out. I knew this gathering was the chance of lifetime to ride alongside legends—true horsemen and cowboys.

As Pa tucked me into bed, he said, "I know you have your heart set on going with us tomorrow, but I want you to understand that your time will come. You will have your chance to ride along with us. Tomorrow is going to be a long day, a day of rough country and wild cattle." As the tears streamed down my face, he told me, "Cowboy up—you will get your chance to sit in the saddle." I buried my head into the pillow to muffle the sounds of a brokenhearted boy. I wondered why I couldn't go. I could ride, I could rope, and I sure wasn't afraid!

I don't know when I fell asleep, but I do remember a nudge and a voice saying, "You better get up, it's time to grab them boots and catch your horse." Was I dreaming? I ran downstairs and into the kitchen, where my mother sat sipping a cup of coffee.

"There's my favorite little cowboy. Come give your mother a hug and promise me you will be safe today and you won't be in the way," she said.

I asked her what had made Pa change his mind. She said, "He just needed someone to ride along with him, someone special. You be sure and tell him thanks for giving you this chance."

When I entered the pen, all I could see were moonlit figures of giants wearing felt hats. There was a thick smell of dust in the air, as the sound of pounding hooves circled around me. Soon, all the mounts were roped out and saddled, and I led my horse out of the gate, feeling like I was among kings.

Cinches were pulled tight and hats pulled down as we paused in silence for a moment. In the still of the darkness, with my father by my side, I heard him say, "Fellers, we all have a job, we all have a duty. Let us not forget that we all have someone beside us, someone to help us as we ride along. So, let's cowboy up and get it done!"

It turned out to be a long, hard day, and there were times when I wanted to quit, but I sure didn't let anyone know it. I was so sore the next day I could hardly walk. And I remember Mama saying, "In life and in cooking, we all require love and someone to ride along with."

Whether on the plate or in the pasture, find a partner to complement the meal and the journey down the trail.

Tangy Skillet Green Beans

PREP TIME: **5 minutes**
TOTAL TIME: **20 minutes**
MAKES ABOUT 4 SERVINGS

1 pound fresh green beans, trimmed

2 to 3 cups chicken broth

4 slices thick-cut bacon

½ stick butter

2 teaspoons soy sauce

2 teaspoons balsamic vinegar

½ teaspoon garlic powder

Coarse sea salt

I'm a fan of the traditional bacon-and-butter green beans. But these fellers have a subtle tang and unique blend of flavors. Looking for a new way to serve your green beans? I highly suggest this recipe. The beans are cooked in chicken broth and then tossed in a soy and balsamic vinegar sauce for a little tartness that mellows with added butter. They are finished off with coarse sea salt and chopped bacon.

---

1. Put the green beans in a large skillet and fill about halfway with the chicken broth. Bring to a low boil and cook, stirring occasionally, just until tender, about 10 minutes.

2. Meanwhile, cook the bacon in a medium skillet over medium-high heat, turning, until crispy, about 8 minutes. Let cool on a paper towel, then chop and set aside.

3. Melt the butter in a small saucepan over medium heat. Stir in the soy sauce, balsamic vinegar, and garlic powder and cook, stirring occasionally, for 2 minutes, to allow the flavors to blend.

4. Drain any excess broth from the green beans. Pour the soy sauce mixture over the beans and toss to coat. Sprinkle with coarse sea salt, top with the chopped bacon, and serve.

Copper Pennies

PREP TIME: **5 minutes**

TOTAL TIME: **20 minutes**

MAKES ABOUT 6 SERVINGS

2 pounds carrots, peeled and sliced into ¼-inch-thick rounds

1 stick butter, cubed

1¼ cups packed light brown sugar

You don't have to serve something fancy to dazzle folks, you just need to cook from the heart. With a few simple ingredients, you can transform plain carrots into something special, as I did with these on Food Network's Chopped Grill Masters. *Carrots are thinly sliced, boiled tender, and then coated with brown sugar and butter, which cooks down to a glaze.*

—◆—

1. In a medium saucepan, cover the carrots with water. Bring to a boil and cook just until tender, about 5 minutes.

2. Drain the water and return the pan to the stove. Stir in the butter and cook over medium heat, stirring occasionally, until the butter melts.

3. Stir in the brown sugar and simmer over low heat, stirring occasionally, for about 5 minutes, until the carrots are tender and the sauce thickens slightly. Serve.

There is only one job I know for sure where you can start at the top, and that is digging holes.

Bacon-Baked Cabbage

PREP TIME: **5 minutes**
TOTAL TIME: **45 minutes**
MAKES 4 TO 6 SERVINGS

1 head green cabbage
5 slices thick-cut bacon
2 teaspoons minced garlic
Salt and black pepper
Smoked paprika
½ stick butter

Butter and bacon are the stars of the show in this dish. Baked down with the cabbage in a good iron skillet, they give the cabbage a warm, savory taste. At the end, we fry up some extra cabbage leaves and sprinkle them on top before serving for a little char and crunch.

1. Preheat the oven to 375°F with a rack in the lower third.

2. Remove 4 of the outer leaves of the cabbage and set aside. Coarsely chop the remaining cabbage.

3. Chop 2 slices of the bacon and add to a 12-inch cast-iron skillet. Cook over medium-high heat, stirring, until crispy, about 8 minutes. Remove the bacon pieces with a slotted spoon, drain on a paper towel, and set aside. Reserve the grease in the skillet.

4. Stir the chopped cabbage into the skillet with the reserved bacon grease. Stir in the garlic. Cut the remaining 3 strips bacon into 1-inch pieces and arrange them evenly on top of the cabbage. Season with salt, pepper, and smoked paprika to taste.

5. Bake for about 40 minutes, until the cabbage is tender. About 30 minutes into the baking time, add 3 tablespoons of the butter and continue baking.

6. Meanwhile, melt the remaining 1 tablespoon butter in a small skillet over medium-high heat. Chop the reserved cabbage leaves, add to the skillet, and cook until charred, about 3 minutes, stirring frequently.

7. Remove the skillet from the oven and sprinkle the charred cabbage and cooked bacon on top. Serve.

OUTDOOR COOKING TIP

When cooking in a Dutch oven with coals, start with slightly heavier heat around the bottom for more even cooking.

Mama's Cheesy Squash Bake

PREP TIME: **20 minutes**

TOTAL TIME: **45 minutes**

MAKES ABOUT 6 SERVINGS

¾ stick butter, melted

5 medium yellow squash, sliced ¼-inch thick (about 7 cups)

1 medium yellow onion, chopped

Salt and black pepper

2 large eggs

½ cup mayonnaise

½ cup milk

1 cup shredded cheddar cheese

1 cup shredded mozzarella cheese

1 sleeve saltine or Ritz crackers, crumbled

½ cup shredded or grated Parmesan cheese

This was on our table many a Sunday after church in the summertime. Mama always knew how to take a few simple ingredients and make them into a homemade masterpiece. Tender squash is blended with mozzarella and cheddar cheeses and topped with a crushed-cracker crust.

———◆———

1. Preheat the oven to 350°F. Butter a 12-inch cast-iron skillet or 9-x-13-inch casserole dish.

2. Heat 3 tablespoons of the butter in a large skillet over medium-high heat. Add the squash and onion, season lightly with salt and pepper, and cook, stirring occasionally, until the squash is tender, about 10 minutes.

3. Remove from the heat and drain the squash and onion well in a colander. Transfer to a large bowl.

4. In a medium bowl, whisk together the eggs, mayonnaise, milk, and cheddar and mozzarella cheeses.

5. Lightly stir the egg and cheese mixture into the squash mixture. Scrape the cheesy squash into the prepared skillet or casserole dish. Sprinkle the top with the crumbled crackers, followed by the Parmesan cheese. Evenly pour the remaining 3 tablespoons butter on top.

6. Bake for about 25 minutes, or until the casserole sets up and is lightly browned on top. Serve hot.

TIP

It's important to drain the squash well after cooking to prevent it from becoming too mushy.

*Faith does not make things easy,
it makes them possible.*

— Luke 1:37

Southern Fried Green 'Maters

PREP TIME: **15 minutes**

TOTAL TIME: **30 minutes**

MAKES ABOUT 6 SERVINGS

2 large green tomatoes

⅓ cup sugar for sprinkling

Black pepper

1 cup cornmeal mix

1 cup all-purpose flour

2 teaspoons paprika or smoked paprika

1 teaspoon garlic powder

1 teaspoon salt

1 (5-ounce) bag seasoned croutons, finely crushed

1 large egg

1 cup buttermilk

Peanut or canola oil for frying

I've always felt richer counting my blessings instead of my money.

This is a Southern delicacy, and there are a few tricks that go into making these treats taste so good. I like to pick tomatoes that aren't completely green but have a little red coloring around them so they aren't too tart. I also like to sprinkle just a bit of sugar on them before coating. Finally, I pat on a good crust made out of crushed seasoned croutons. So, whether you get your tomatoes from your own garden or go steal some from the neighbors, give these a try!

————◆————

1. Slice the tomatoes about ¼-inch thick and set on a paper towel. Sprinkle both sides of each tomato slice with about 1 teaspoon of the sugar, then with some black pepper. Cover with a paper towel and let sit for 10 minutes.

2. In a large, shallow bowl, combine the cornmeal mix, ½ cup of the flour, 2 teaspoons black pepper, the paprika, garlic powder, and salt.

3. In another shallow bowl, combine the crouton crumbs and the remaining ½ cup flour. In a third bowl, whisk together the egg and buttermilk.

4. In a large cast-iron skillet, heat about ½ inch of oil to 350°F.

5. Remove the paper towel from the tomatoes and sprinkle each one lightly with another ½ teaspoon sugar. Skip this step if you like a tarter tomato.

6. Dredge each tomato slice in the buttermilk mixture, followed by the cornmeal mix, to generously coat. Dip them back through the buttermilk mix and finish by dredging in the crushed croutons. Lightly pat the crumb mixture on both sides so it sticks before frying.

TIP

These can also be deep-fried for a crunchier texture.

7. Add the tomatoes to the skillet, a few at a time, and fry for 1 to 2 minutes per side, until crispy and golden brown. Remove from the oil with a slotted spatula and let cool slightly on a wire rack. Serve hot.

Crispy Onion Rings

PREP TIME: **15 minutes**
TOTAL TIME: **25 minutes**
MAKES ABOUT 6 TO 8 SERVINGS

2 cups all-purpose flour

1 tablespoon cornstarch

2 teaspoons garlic powder

2 teaspoons salt

2 teaspoons black pepper

2 teaspoons baking powder

About 2 cups panko bread crumbs

2 cups buttermilk

2 teaspoons paprika or smoked paprika

2 large Vidalia or yellow onions, sliced into ¼- to ½-inch-thick rings

Peanut or canola oil for frying

I judge a burger shack by how good their onion rings are, and I've eaten a lot of them in my time. I sure don't like a soggy ring. We fry these up in a buttermilk batter, seasoned flour, and panko bread crumbs, which gives them a good crunch in every bite. We like to use a Vidalia onion for a little sweetness, but a regular onion will also work. Try these with Chipotle Aioli Sauce (page 163).

———◆———

1. In a medium bowl, combine the flour, cornstarch, garlic powder, salt, pepper, and baking powder.

2. Put the bread crumbs in a shallow dish. In another shallow dish, whisk together the buttermilk and paprika.

3. Dip each onion ring in the buttermilk, then dredge in the flour mixture. Dip back in the buttermilk and finish dredging through the bread crumbs, until the rings are well coated.

4. In a large saucepan or Dutch oven, heat 3 to 4 inches of oil to 350°F. Add a few of the rings at a time and fry, turning frequently, until golden brown, 3 to 4 minutes. Remove from the oil with a slotted spatula and let cool slightly on a wire rack. Serve hot.

It's better to be thankful for what you have than to wish for more than you need.

Riding for the Brand

Branding livestock has been around a long time, even back to the Egyptians in 2700 BC, though I sure can't picture King Tut in a cowboy hat. Branding is typically done in the spring months as a way to identify cattle as being owned by a particular ranch. Branding time also generally includes vaccinations, pregnancy checking, and other preventive measures.

A traditional branding iron is heated over an open fire or a propane torch, but the industry has modernized to include freeze branding, which is done with liquid nitrogen, or an electric iron, with no fire needed. Whatever the method, the outcome is still the same. The hide is marked, and when done right, that symbol will stand the test of time.

Branding is an art. It takes a steady hand and good crew to make sure this mark by fire and steel is there to stay. If you're in too big a hurry and pull that iron off too quickly, the mark can just peel off. It's like anything else in life: If we get too busy and don't pay attention, our work isn't solid and we damage our brand.

Signing on to work for a cow outfit is called "riding for the brand." When a cowboy rides for the brand, he's pledging to take care of the livestock and carry out all his duties. But it goes far beyond performing specific tasks for a ranch. It's about taking pride in what you do, not asking for more than you deserve, and letting your actions speak louder than words. A brand is not only a mark of ownership but also stands for what we represent.

We've all been branded in one way or another—branded by the way we were reared and the choices we make. We are also branded by the things that we value, like family and faith. Our brand shows in the way we treat others. It should be a visible sign to those around us of what we stand for. Your brand and your word go hand in hand.

There will be many things in life that will try to tarnish your brand and challenge what you stand for. Fear and doubt will try to cover your mark at times. But if it's solid, your brand will outlast time and the elements. Remember you have a reputation and legacy to live up to, forged by those who came before us.

What's your brand? What do you stand for?

Green Onion and Ham Scalloped Potatoes

PREP TIME: 15 minutes

TOTAL TIME: 1 hour 20 minutes

MAKES 8 SERVINGS

3½ cups milk

3 tablespoons butter

¼ cup all-purpose flour

1 (16-ounce) tub green onion or French onion dip

5 russet potatoes, peeled and cut into ⅛- to ¼-inch-thick rounds

2 cups chopped cooked ham

2 cups shredded mozzarella cheese

1 cup shredded Parmesan cheese

Salt and black pepper

Chopped green onions for topping

OUTDOOR COOKING TIP

When using wood or hardwood lump charcoal with a Dutch oven, bring the dish to a good simmer with top and bottom heat for 10 to 15 minutes. Remove from the bottom heat to prevent burning and finish cooking with top heat only.

A good scalloped potato recipe is a staple at any community, family, or church gathering. Shannon adds layers of mozzarella and Parmesan cheese, chunks of ham, and—her own distinctive spin—green onion dip. Your crowd won't be disappointed when you bring this to the next social.

————◆————

1. Preheat the oven to 400°F. Lightly grease a 12-inch cast-iron skillet or 9-x-13-inch casserole dish.

2. Warm the milk and butter in a large saucepan over medium heat until the butter has melted. Add the flour and cook just until it thickens to a thin gravy, 2 to 3 minutes, stirring frequently.

3. Remove from the heat and stir in the onion dip until smooth.

4. Arrange half the potatoes in the skillet or dish. Pour half the milk mixture on top. Sprinkle with 1 cup of the ham, 1 cup of the mozzarella, and ½ cup of the Parmesan. Season with salt and pepper to taste. Repeat the layers once more.

5. Cover with foil and bake for 45 minutes. Remove the foil and continue baking for another 20 minutes, or until the potatoes soften and the cheese has slightly browned. You can brown the cheese more by broiling for a couple of minutes or moving the skillet to the top oven rack at the end of baking. Top with chopped green onions and serve.

Loaded Tater Bombs

PREP TIME: 20 minutes
TOTAL TIME: 35 minutes
MAKES 8 POTATO BALLS

3½ cups mashed potatoes

⅓ cup bacon bits (store-bought or fresh-cooked)

⅓ cup diced green onion

Salt and black pepper

½ to ¾ cup all-purpose flour, plus more for dusting

About ¼ cup sour cream

⅓ cup shredded cheddar cheese

1 large egg, beaten

2 cups panko bread crumbs

Peanut or canola oil for frying

Don't ever wonder what you're going to do with those left-over mashed potatoes anymore, though it's worth making them just so you can have them for this dish. These fellers are packed with layers of flavor. They're mixed with green onions, bacon bits, cheddar cheese, and sour cream and then deep-fried. Panko bread crumbs give the perfect outer crust for a crunch.

———— •–• ————

1. In a large bowl, stir the potatoes until smooth. Stir in the bacon bits and green onion; season with salt and pepper to taste.

2. Stir in enough flour so the potatoes hold together and aren't sticky. Reserve about ⅓ cup of the potatoes for coating the potato balls later. Flour your hands and roll the remaining mashed potatoes into 8 balls.

3. Form a deep well in the middle of each of the balls with your finger. Layer in a heaping teaspoon of the sour cream, followed by 1 to 2 teaspoons of the cheddar cheese.

4. Bring the outside edges of the potato balls together to seal at the top. Add some of the reserved ⅓ cup of potatoes to the top to seal, if needed.

5. Brush the balls with the egg and generously coat with the bread crumbs.

6. In a large saucepan or Dutch oven, heat 3 to 4 inches of oil to 350°F. Add a few of the potato balls at a time and deep-fry, turning frequently, until golden brown, 3 to 4 minutes. Remove from the oil with a slotted spoon and let cool slightly on a wire rack. Serve hot.

Root Beer–Roasted Potatoes and Caramelized Onions

PREP TIME: **15 minutes**

TOTAL TIME: **55 minutes**

MAKES 4 TO 6 SERVINGS

1 (1½-pound) bag baby or mini potatoes (red or yellow)

2 large garlic cloves, minced

3 to 4 cups root beer

Salt and black pepper

1 large yellow onion, cut into ⅛- to ¼-inch-thick rings

Folks, I like to blend ingredients that you might not think go together. We start off with mini potatoes—you can choose whichever style you like—and add a little garlic. The magic ingredient is the root beer. Even if you don't like root beer, give this recipe a try. The soda nearly cooks off and you're left with a subtle vanilla, caramel-like flavor. While those cook up, we caramelize some onions in the root beer, which we serve with the potatoes or on top of our Perfect 10-Minute Beef Filet (page 194).

1. Preheat the oven to 375°F. Butter a 10-inch Dutch oven or cast-iron skillet.

2. Slice the potatoes in half and place them in the Dutch oven or dish. Stir in half the minced garlic. Pour in enough of the root beer to reach about halfway up the potatoes. Cover and let rest for 10 to 15 minutes.

3. Bake for about 40 minutes, or until the potatoes are tender. Season with salt and pepper to taste.

4. Meanwhile, add the onion and remaining minced garlic to a medium cast-iron skillet. Stir in ½ cup of the root beer. Cook over medium heat, stirring occasionally, until the onions soften and the root beer reduces to about half, about 10 minutes. Serve on top of the potatoes.

OUTDOOR COOKING TIP

When cooking with coals in a Dutch oven, you may need to add a little more root beer while cooking so it doesn't entirely cook off and the potatoes become dry.

Ranch Refried Beans

PREP TIME: **5 minutes**
TOTAL TIME: **3 hours**
MAKES 6 TO 8 SERVINGS

1 pound dried pinto beans

4 slices thick-cut bacon, cut into ½-inch pieces

1 medium yellow onion, chopped

2 fresh cayenne chiles, stemmed, seeded, and chopped

2 medium dried ancho chiles, stemmed, seeded, and chopped

1 teaspoon salt

1 teaspoon black pepper

1 teaspoon garlic powder

½ stick butter

½ cup mayonnaise

½ cup sour cream

1 teaspoon ground cumin

1 teaspoon smoked paprika

Finely chopped green onions and shredded cheese (such as cheddar, pepper jack, or queso fresco) for serving (optional)

TIPS

We prefer the Casserole brand of beans.

Save the broth from the boiled beans and add to soups or use to baste a roast or pork chops.

To me, the sign of a good Mexican restaurant is how well they make refried beans. We're not going with the canned version here, folks! This is inspired by a traditional refried bean recipe with mashed pinto beans, not whipped, for a hearty texture and Mexican spices for flavor. We're adding our cowboy flair by mixing in sour cream and mayonnaise for creaminess. This can be served as a side dish or with tortilla chips as a dip.

1. In a large pot, cover the beans with 1½ to 2 inches of hot water. Bring to a boil over high heat, then stir in the bacon, onion, and cayenne and ancho chiles. Cover and continue to boil for about 10 minutes.

2. Stir in the salt, pepper, garlic powder, and 2 tablespoons of the butter. Reduce the heat to a low boil, cover, and continue cooking for 2 to 2½ hours, until the beans are slightly tender. Be sure the beans stay covered with about 1½ inches of water while cooking, and be sure to add hot water to the beans as needed. Drain well in a colander. For high elevation cooking, you will need to increase the cooking time up to 3 to 4 hours.

3. In a large cast-iron skillet, melt the remaining 2 tablespoons butter over medium-low heat. Add the beans and mash with a potato masher until smooth but with some texture.

4. Stir in the mayonnaise, sour cream, cumin, and smoked paprika and cook, stirring occasionally, until heated through, about 5 minutes. Serve topped with green onions and cheese, if desired.

Spinach, Rice, and Mushroom Bake

PREP TIME: **20 minutes**
TOTAL TIME: **40 minutes**
MAKES ABOUT 6 SERVINGS

1 cup white rice

2 tablespoons butter

3 cups stemmed, thinly sliced white mushrooms

4 cups finely chopped fresh spinach

½ cup milk

5 large eggs

2 tablespoons Worcestershire sauce

1 teaspoon garlic powder

1 teaspoon onion powder

Salt and black pepper

⅓ cup shredded Parmesan cheese

We sauté mushrooms just long enough to help release the flavors and toss them with fresh spinach, rice, and Worcestershire sauce for a bit of a tang. Whisked eggs bind this all together, and the final topping is shredded Parmesan cheese. This is an easy way to transform vegetables into a tasty meal, or it can double as a side.

1. Preheat the oven to 350°F. Butter a 9-inch square baking dish or 10-inch cast-iron skillet.

2. Prepare the rice as directed on the box.

3. Meanwhile, melt the butter in a medium skillet over medium heat. Stir in the mushrooms and cook, stirring occasionally, just until the color changes and the flavors begin to release, 3 to 5 minutes.

4. Scrape the mushrooms into a large bowl. Stir in the spinach and cooked rice.

5. In a medium bowl, whisk together the milk, eggs, Worcestershire sauce, garlic powder, onion powder, and 1 teaspoon each salt and pepper. Pour into the spinach mixture and stir to combine.

6. Scrape the mixture into the baking dish or skillet and sprinkle the Parmesan cheese on top. Bake for about 20 minutes, until the eggs are set and an inserted knife comes out clean. Season with salt and pepper and serve.

Green Chile Mac and Cheese

PREP TIME: **25 minutes**
TOTAL TIME: **25 minutes**
MAKES 6 TO 8 SERVINGS

3 cups elbow macaroni (uncooked)

6 slices thick-cut bacon

½ stick butter

¼ cup all-purpose flour

2½ cups milk

2½ teaspoons garlic powder

2½ cups shredded sharp cheddar cheese

1 or 2 (4-ounce) can(s) chopped green chiles, drained

Salt and black pepper

Southwest flavor joins forces with a comfort-food classic. Shannon has always been a connoisseur of mac and cheese, but she went above and beyond on this dish. The sharp cheddar melts down and blends well with the green chiles, which give it just a little kick. And of course, everything is better with a little bacon in it!

1. In a large pot of salted boiling water, cook the macaroni over high heat just until tender, 8 to 10 minutes. Drain and return the macaroni back to the pot.

2. Meanwhile, brown the bacon in a large skillet over medium-high heat, turning once, until crispy, about 8 minutes. Let cool on a paper towel, then chop.

3. Melt the butter in a large saucepan over medium heat. Stir in the flour until smooth. Slowly pour in the milk and continue to cook, stirring frequently, until it thickens just slightly, 2 to 3 minutes .

4. Stir in the garlic powder, then the cheese, and continue stirring until melted. Stir in 1 or 2 cans of green chiles, depending on how spicy you like it. Stir in the chopped bacon and salt and pepper to taste. Continue to cook for a few minutes more, until all the ingredients have warmed through, stirring frequently.

5. Pour the cheese mixture over the macaroni and stir until thoroughly coated. Season again to taste, if needed, and serve.

TIP
Add a little of the bacon grease from the skillet to the cheese mixture to add more bacon flavor.

> ## I've been paid in money, which I quickly spent. But pay me in friendship, and I will always be wealthy.

Baptized by Bertha

Grilling

For those of you who haven't met Bertha, she is our 385-pound camp stove. In the words of Elvis, she's a "hunk of burning love." She has seen it all, from ranches to parking lots to mountaintops. Fueled by mesquite, this old iron gal has turned out many a tender grilled dish.

Bertha has taught plenty of folks a lesson, from "You've done stayed too long" to "No, you cannot set that there." She has welcomed cowboys into camp on a cool morning and run some off when it was 110 degrees in August. During one festival, a feller waltzed right into camp without an invitation and began telling us how good a chef he was. I'm pretty sure the only place he hadn't cooked was on the moon. When he finished, I said, "You reckon you could come out at noon to help us grill a hundred steaks? I bet you would be just the man for the job."

"Yep," he replied, "I could probably teach you two a little something about grilling meat."

This man of too many words was wearing a pair of Moodar shorts (that's short for Bermuda shorts) and flip-flops. It was 91 degrees in the shade that day and the humidity was about 95 percent. It didn't take long before this know-it-all was backing up faster than a runaway dump truck going downhill. His face got red, and then those flip-flops began to curl up at the toes like bacon in hot grease. I could tell he was looking for a chance to break and run.

He lasted about fifteen minutes before he threw in the spatula and hightailed it out of there, smoking a little around the edges. And that's the last we saw of him—just another lucky one that got baptized by Bertha's fire!

These recipes have been cowboy tested and Bertha approved, so fire up your grills!

Caveman Steak

PREP TIME: **30 minutes**
TOTAL TIME: **45 minutes**
MAKES 2 SERVINGS

2 ears sweet corn, in the husks

Juice of 1 lime

2 (14-ounce) rib eye steaks

Salt and black pepper

1 bell pepper (green, red, yellow, or orange)

¾ stick butter

1 tablespoon minced garlic

½ tablespoon prepared horseradish

¼ cup white wine, plus more if desired (we like Hatch Green Chile Wine)

We've had more than one million views of this on our You-Tube channel, because it's such a great way to cook a steak. Instead of using the grill, we dig a hole in the ground and build a fire in it. We cook the steak directly on those coals, which gives a better sear to the meat and locks in moisture and flavor. We finish that all in a horseradish and white wine sauce for a little extra bite of flavor. Since you've got the fire hot, go ahead and add corn and a bell pepper to serve along-side the steak.

———— •◆• ————

1. Dig a hole in the ground about 2 feet long x 10 inches wide x 10 inches deep. Fill the hole with hardwood or hardwood lump charcoal. Light the coals and let them burn down until they are nearly all white. Be sure to fan the coals well before cooking, which will remove any loose ash.

2. Meanwhile, in a large bowl, cover the corn with water. Let soak for 20 minutes.

3. Generously rub lime juice on one side of the steaks. Season with salt and pepper to taste and rub in well. Flip over and repeat on the other side. Cover and let sit for about 15 minutes.

4. Set the corn, bell pepper, and steaks directly on the coals. Cook the vegetables, turning occasionally, until the pepper is charred and the corn softens, 8 to 10 minutes for the corn and 4 to 5 minutes for the pepper. Cook the steaks for about 3 minutes per side. Remove from the heat and keep warm.

Fanning the coals before cooking will remove most of the ash. However, if a little still clings to the steaks, simply brush it off and serve.

5. Meanwhile, place the butter, garlic, and horseradish in a large cast-iron skillet. Set on the coals and cook, stirring frequently, until the butter has melted and just slightly browned. Stir in the white wine. Place the steaks in the skillet and cook for 1 to 2 minutes per side. For more flavor, you can add a splash more of the wine while cooking, if desired.

6. Let the steaks rest for a few minutes before cutting. Drizzle the wine sauce over the steaks and serve immediately, with the corn and bell pepper.

MASTERING THE FIRE
Grilling Tips

I've been around a lot of fires in my time: the branding fire, the campfire, and, of course, the grilling fire. I've never had a high-dollar grill. One of my first ones was two cinder blocks and a grate out of an old refrigerator. Grilling isn't rocket science, or else I sure wouldn't do it. I'll let you in on a few tips, and if you're a pro, well, you can always learn a few new tricks to try out the next time you're cooking for the neighbors. From *Chopped Grill Masters* to remote camps in the middle of 300,000 acres, every fire has taught me a lesson and every steak has created a memory. So, let's keep the wood dry and the fire hot!

Don't use lighter fuel. Raise your right hand and repeat after me: I promise never to use lighter fuel when grilling—ever. I can't stress this enough. I want to taste the meat, not a shot of rocket fuel. Lighter fluid will give your steaks an artificial flavor and can even make some folks sick. Switch to one of the more natural methods below.

Start your fire the right way. We've come a long way from rubbing two sticks together. There are two methods I prefer to start a fire: a propane torch or a chimney. You can buy a torch (weed burner) that attaches to a propane tank that will set things blazing quickly. There are even smaller handheld versions too. The chimney starter is another good choice. Crumple two or three pages of newspaper (black-and-white, not colored ink), put them in the bottom of the chimney, fill the rest with lump coals, and light the paper. When the flame reaches the top, pour the contents out onto the bottom of the grill and then wait for them to turn white before grilling.

Try a hardwood lump charcoal instead of briquettes. Like lighter fluid, briquettes are full of additives and will alter the flavor of your meat. Hardwood lump charcoal is made from real wood that has been burned down. It offers great flavor in a variety of different types of wood. Hardwood lump charcoal provides a much more consistent and hotter heat. It is also great for Dutch oven cooking.

Marinate in lime and lemon juices. I don't like to mask the natural flavor of meat, but rather enhance it. Rub lime juice on the meat (beef, pork, and wild game) along with your favorite seasonings, cover, and marinate for about four hours. The acid in the juice will help break down the muscle fibers for a more tender steak without overpowering its flavor. Use lemon juice when preparing anything with fins or feathers.

Set up a hot side and a cool side. Depending on the style of your grill, you may benefit from having a hot (direct) and cool (indirect) side of the fire. Bertha, for example, doesn't have different height grates nor a knob to regulate heat. I like to have a cooler side of the fire for warming foods up before I go straight to the hot side or if I need to slow down the cooking.

Use foil when grilling pork or chicken. Pork and chicken tend to dry out on a grill. I like to wrap them in foil (add a little butter with chicken) and grill over high heat for about 5 minutes per side. Remove the foil and finish directly on the grill. The steaming in the foil before grilling will help retain moisture.

THE TOUCH TEST
How to Tell When Your Steak Is Done

I've never been one to use a thermometer when cooking steak, because my preferred method is by touch. After you get a few steaks under your belt, you'll know just what to feel for to grill a steak just the way you like it.

Lightly touch your thumb and index finger together. With your opposite hand, feel the meaty part of your palm, at the base of your thumb; you'll notice a soft palm with some give. This indicates how a rare steak will feel.

Now touch your middle finger to your thumb. The slightly firmer feel of the palm indicates how a medium-cooked steak will feel. Your ring finger to the thumb signifies a medium-well steak, and finally, pinky to thumb is similar to how a well-done steak will feel.

The more a steak cooks, the tighter the muscle will become, as demonstrated as you move through your fingers from index to pinky. The muscle gets tighter and tougher, as will your steak. If you want my advice, I'd go ahead and cut those last two fingers off, 'cause I'm not going to cook a steak past medium—cooking longer will cause it to lose both flavor and tenderness.

FUEL THE FIRE!

Types of Wood for Your Outdoor Cooking

Archaeologists say that fire may predate modern man by some 800,000 years. So, as we say in my country, that's older than dinosaur dirt! Here is a quick reference guide to some popular types of wood, what type of coal and heat they produce, and when they're best used for grilling and Dutch oven cooking. »—▶

Wood	Coal Quality	Heat	Notes
Bois d'Arc (aka Osage Orange, Hedge, Horse Apple)	Excellent	High	This wood creates a very live and sparking fire. Be careful in windy and drought conditions or when cooking in a Dutch oven. Not recommended for grilling.
Mesquite	Excellent	High	Found in the Southwest. My favorite all-purpose wood. Has great flavor for grilling and a long, hot cooking time.
Oak (Red, White, Black, Blackjack, Post, Live)	Good to Excellent	Moderate to High	Easily found throughout the U.S. A good choice for all-purpose grilling and Dutch oven cooking.
Hickory	Decent	Moderate to High	Hickory is often used for smoking and can give a bold flavor. Pairs well with pork and chicken.
Pecan	Fair	High	Good smoking wood.
Cedar	Fair	High	It creates a high heat but ashes out quickly and produces a lot of smoke. Not recommended for grilling.
Pine	Poor	Low	High resin creates a lot of smoke. Not recommended for grilling or Dutch oven cooking.
Pinion/Cottonwood/ Water Oak	Poor	Low	Not recommended.
Fruit Woods (Cherry, Peach, Apple)	Fair	Moderate	Softer woods are not recommended for Dutch oven cooking, because of their low coal quality. However, they are good for grilling because they add great flavor and are recommended when grilling fins or feathers.

Mexican Steak Fajitas

PREP TIME: 6 hours and 10 minutes
TOTAL TIME: 6 hours and
30 minutes
MAKES ABOUT 6 SERVINGS

¼ cup chili powder

2 tablespoons ground cumin

1½ tablespoons coarse
sea salt

1½ tablespoons coarsely
ground black pepper

1 tablespoon smoked paprika

1 tablespoon ancho chile
powder

2 teaspoons ground oregano

1 teaspoon garlic powder

1 teaspoon red pepper flakes

2 to 2½ pounds skirt steak

Lime juice

3 bell peppers (1 yellow, 1 red,
1 orange)

2 jalapeños

1 large yellow onion

¼ cup water

Flour tortillas, store-bought
or Easy Homemade Tortillas
(page 110), shredded cheese,
and sour cream for serving

Skirt steak has a distinct beefy flavor, and it can be less expensive than some of its cousins. It can also be a little tough, so I marinate it overnight with lime juice and a seasoning blend full of classic Mexican spices. Then I finish it by simmering in a skillet with charred-on-the-grill veggies. For maximal tenderness, be sure to cut against the grain. Serve with our homemade tortillas for a special addition.

———— •◆• ————

1. Make the seasoning blend by combining the chili powder, cumin, sea salt, black pepper, smoked paprika, ancho chile powder, oregano, garlic powder, and red pepper flakes in a small bowl.

2. Rub one side of the steak with lime juice. Generously sprinkle with the seasoning blend and rub in well. Flip the steak and repeat on the other side. Reserve about 1 tablespoon of the seasoning blend.

3. Put the steak in a zippertop bag and refrigerate for at least 6 hours or overnight. Remove from the fridge about 30 minutes before grilling.

4. Meanwhile, clean, oil, and preheat the grill to medium-high. Cut the bell peppers and jalapeños in half and remove the seeds. Cut the onion in half. Grill the vegetables, turning frequently, until tender and lightly charred, about 3 minutes per side. Close the lid while grilling to enhance the smoky flavor. Remove from the heat, let cool slightly, and slice into strips. Set aside in a warm place.

It's a great day above the grass.

5. Grill the steak over medium-high with the lid closed for about 2 minutes per side. Remove from the grill and let rest for a few minutes, then slice into thin strips at an angle against the grain.

6. Add the steak strips, vegetables, the 1 tablespoon reserved seasoning blend, and the ¼ cup water to a 12-inch cast-iron skillet. Simmer on the grill or stovetop, stirring occasionally, for about 20 minutes, to allow the flavors to incorporate. Serve with tortillas, shredded cheese, and sour cream.

Cowboy-Style Philly Cheesesteaks

PREP TIME: **4 hours**

TOTAL TIME: **4 hours and 25 minutes**

MAKES 6 SERVINGS

Lime juice

2½ to 3 pounds skirt or flank steak

2 tablespoons meat tenderizer

Salt and black pepper

2 bell peppers (1 green, 1 red)

1 large yellow onion

2 tablespoons butter, melted, plus more for the rolls

6 hoagie rolls

Cheese Sauce (opposite)

To have a great meal, it doesn't take fancy frills; it takes good meat, good friends, and hot grills.

Don't hitch the wagon up and drive all the way to Philadelphia for this one, 'cause we're doing this cowboy style. I use skirt or flank steak because they have great flavor and typically cost less than the rib eye. I let the steak marinate for at least four hours. My favorite part of this dish is the cheese sauce. We use provolone, which has a light, natural smoke flavor, with a little horseradish for some zest.

------◆◆------

1. Rub lime juice on one side of the steak. Sprinkle with 1 tablespoon of the meat tenderizer and rub it in, followed by salt and pepper. Flip and repeat on the other side. Cover and refrigerate for 4 hours; remove 30 minutes before grilling.

2. Meanwhile, clean, oil, and preheat the grill to medium-high. Cut the bell peppers into large pieces and remove the seeds and veins. Cut the onion into large slices.

3. Grill the veggies and steak until the steak is medium rare to medium and the vegetables are tender and slightly charred, 2 minutes per side for the steak and 2 to 3 minutes for the veggies. Press the veggies down slightly while grilling for more even cooking. Remove from the heat and let cool enough to handle.

4. Chop the veggies and place them in a large cast-iron skillet with the butter. Chop the steak and stir it in with the veggies. Simmer over medium-low heat for about 10 minutes, stirring occasionally.

5. Butter the inside of the hoagie rolls and grill them butter side down over medum heat until toasted.

6. Spoon the meat and veggies into the hoagies, top with cheese sauce, and serve.

Cheese Sauce

PREP TIME: 10 minutes
TOTAL TIME: 10 minutes
MAKES ABOUT 2⅓ CUPS

2 tablespoons butter

¼ cup all-purpose flour

2 cups milk, plus more if needed

8 ounces provolone cheese

1½ to 2 tablespoons prepared horseradish

1. In a medium saucepan, melt the butter over medium heat. Stir in the flour until smooth.

2. Stir in the milk and cook, stirring frequently, until thickened to a creamy consistency, 3 to 5 minutes. Tear the provolone into pieces or cut into chunks, slowly add it to the mixture, and cook, stirring, until smooth and melted, 2 to 3 minutes.

3. Stir in the horseradish to taste. If needed, slowly add more milk, about a tablespoon at a time, just until the cheese sauce is pourable. Pour over the cheesesteaks.

Smoked Texas Toast Cheeseburgers with Chipotle Aioli Sauce

PREP TIME: 10 minutes
TOTAL TIME: 30 minutes
MAKES 4 BURGERS

2 pounds ground beef
(80% lean)

Salt and black pepper

4 jalapeños, halved and
seeded

4 slices cheddar cheese

½ stick butter, softened

8 slices Texas toast or other
thick-cut bread

Parmesan cheese for
sprinkling

4 slices provolone cheese

Lettuce, tomato, and onion
for serving

Chipotle Aioli Sauce
(opposite)

What's a great way to get more flavor from a burger? Smoke it. I like to use hickory chips, but choose any type of wood you like. These burgers are topped with two cheeses and a blistered jalapeño, then served on Texas toast for extra crunch. Layer the burger with any kind of toppings you like and then give it a good drizzle of Chipotle Aioli Sauce for another dab of smoky flavor with a little sweet heat.

—•◆•—

1. Clean and oil the grill and move all the coals to one side. Preheat the grill.

2. Form the ground beef into 4 patties. Shape the patties into squares that are slightly larger than the bread slices, as they will shrink a bit while grilling. Season with salt and pepper to taste.

3. Place the burgers on the indirect-heat side of the grill. Add a couple handfuls of hickory chips (or wood of your choice) to the coal side of the fire. Shut the lid and smoke the burgers for about 3 minutes per side. Be careful not to mash the burgers with a spatula when cooking, as that releases their juices.

4. Meanwhile, cook the jalapeños on the direct-heat side of the grill, turning occasionally, until softened and blistered, about 2 to 3 minutes. Remove from the grill.

5. Move the burgers to the direct-heat side, shut the lid, and grill for about 2 minutes per side, or until medium to medium-well done. To tell when a burger is close to done: Lightly press the corner of a spatula in the middle of the burger; if the juices run clear, it's about done.

Because hamburger is a processed meat, cook to medium or above for safety, unlike a steak.

For a longer lasting smoke, soak the hickory or wood chips in water for about 20 minutes before adding to the grill.

6. Move the burgers back to indirect heat and top with the cheddar cheese. Close the lid and cook just until the cheese melts slightly.

7. Meanwhile, butter one side of each slice of bread and sprinkle with Parmesan cheese. Place the slices, butter-and-Parmesan side down, on the direct-heat side of the grill. Top 4 bread slices with 1 slice of the Provolone cheese and grill until the bread is lightly toasted and the cheese is slightly melted.

8. Set the burgers on the provolone, add the jalapeños and your favorite toppings, then drizzle with the chipotle sauce. Close the burgers and serve immediately.

PREP TIME: 2 minutes
TOTAL TIME: 2 minutes
MAKES ABOUT ½ CUP

¼ cup mayonnaise

2 tablespoons adobo sauce from a can of chipotle chiles

1 tablespoon honey

2 teaspoons Worcestershire sauce

1 teaspoon garlic powder

1 teaspoon smoked paprika

Salt and black pepper

Chipotle Aioli Sauce

Mix all the ingredients together in a small bowl until smooth. Drizzle over the grilled burgers.

TIP

The adobo sauce is spicy, so adjust to your taste.

High Pockets

When I was little, I met a lot of heroes in my little community. Many of them were just simple folks. But there was something different about this one feller, and the first time I remember seeing him was with my dad at the Adams Cotton Gin.

There was an old wooden bench that sat out front of the gin office. Many a backside of Levi's and overalls had slid across that pine and had polished it to a dull shine. It was notched by countless pocketknives with initials that stood out like a brand on a yearling's hide. It was a stout bench, and a historical marker in my book.

One of those backsides belonged to a tall, gangly feller everyone called High Pockets. He always wore a white button-up shirt underneath a pair of striped overalls, and brogan boots. His shirt was always clean, but it was peppered with pinholes from battles fought with hand-rolled Prince Albert cigarettes. A conductor's-style cap perched on his head, and underneath, his weathered face was leather-tanned from untold hours of sun and sweat. But he always wore a smile, and it was genuine and kind.

When I accompanied my dad to the gin one day, I saw him sitting outside on the bench. "You can go visit with High Pockets, and I'll go in and see about getting some cottonseed to feed them old cows," Pa told me.

"Why do they call him High Pockets?" I asked.

"Well, you'll notice that his overalls are too short. His two hip pockets are a little too far up his back, 'cause he keeps his overall straps cinched up pretty tight. He told me he had to keep them that tight to hold up all his money!" Pa explained.

Not really understanding, I asked, "So, he's rich?"

Pa just grinned. "Yep, rich in wisdom and friends." I was a little confused, because I wasn't sure what you could buy with that kind of wealth.

I approached the bench, trying not to be obvious. I can still remember the sound of his pocketknife as he stroked a pine stick in a continuous rhythm. His strokes were as smooth as a windmill in a summer's breeze. "Young'un, you like to whittle?" he asked. "You know, whittling is like growing up. The knife is the people around you, and they mold you into what you're going to be. There are all kinds of wood to whittle on, and some of them are harder than others. Just like people, softer hearts are easier to shape. But some harder woods are beautiful underneath, and the extra effort is worth it. It's really something to see when you get finished, and to see the change you have made."

I don't remember saying anything, just listening and watching him whittle. My dad had always told me a good listener learns faster than a man who gets kicked by the same mule twice. I sat there mesmerized by this man's voice and smooth movements. High Pockets then took out a Prince Albert can and rolled up a cigarette. As he drew a long breath in, smoke slowly leaked from his mouth as he said, "You come from good stock. It sure is easier to put the finishing touch on a whittling job when it's already been started."

He handed me a small pine stick and an extra pocketknife he had hiding in his overalls. "You need to be careful and not cut yourself with that knife," he instructed. "It'll hurt, and you will remember it. It might even leave a scar, but the work you put into that stick will make up for the pain. When you can transform something with your own hands, you'll understand the hours you've spent were worth something."

I don't even know how much time elapsed since we'd arrived at the gin, but it didn't matter. I liked to hear his voice, and even though I didn't understand all he was trying to tell me at the moment, I wanted to sit and listen to him for hours.

When Pa came out of the gin, he told High Pockets, "I hope this young'un ain't been bending your ear too much."

He looked up at Pa and said, "We've just been whittlin' and listenin'."

On the ride back to the house, Pa asked, "You and ol' High Pockets have a good visit?"

"I didn't say much," I replied. "Just sat there and listened. He sure can whittle."

"You know, that man has shaped a lot of things into something special, both people and sticks," Pa said. "I never heard him ask for nothing, and he's always had something to give no matter the circumstances. He never had to be flashy to draw attention to himself. I reckon his actions always spoke louder than words ever will."

As Pa talked, I just looked down at the pine stick, rubbing it in between my fingers. It wasn't anything but scrap lumber, but I held it like a key that could open any door if I just used it right.

The bench at the cotton gin is gone now, and I never found out High Pockets' real name. But I do remember the things he told me that day and the way he shaped me and that pine during that short time on the bench.

On-the-Grill Cheese Sandwiches

PREP TIME: **10 minutes**

TOTAL TIME: **25 minutes**

MAKES 4 SERVINGS

8 slices bread, preferably Texas toast, thick-cut bread or sourdough

1 to 1½ sticks butter, melted

8 slices American cheese

1 cup shredded cheddar cheese

1 cup shredded pepper jack cheese

1 cup shredded mozzarella cheese

1 or 2 jalapeños, grated

4 to 8 teaspoons garlic powder

4 to 8 tablespoons grated Parmesan cheese

Have you ever wondered why it's called a grilled cheese sandwich, when it's hardly ever cooked on the grill? We're taking this comfort food classic and grilling it to create a crunchier texture. The star, of course, is cheese, and we're using four different kinds. I did my homework and found the perfect cheeses to create that gooey meltiness that you want in a cheese sandwich. For a little zing, we top it with grated jalapeño.

———◆———

1. Clean, oil, and preheat the grill to hot, then turn it to low. If you don't have a top rack on your grill, skip the step of preheating to hot and just turn to low.

2. Brush one side of each bread slice generously with butter. Place the slices, buttered side down, on the top rack of the grill or, if your grill doesn't have a top rack, directly on the grill.

3. Brush the top of each slice with butter and grill until a light crust forms on the bottom of the bread, 2 to 3 minutes. Flip the slices over.

4. Top each slice with 1 piece of American cheese. Top 4 of the slices with ¼ cup each of the cheddar, pepper jack, and mozzarella cheeses. Top these 4 slices with grated jalapeño.

5. Assemble the sandwiches by placing the slices with the American cheese on the slices with the shredded cheeses. Close the lid (see Tip), and grill for 2½ to 3 minutes, to allow the cheeses to melt.

6. Brush the top of the sandwiches with more butter and flip over. Close the lid and grill for another 2 minutes.

TIP

If your grill doesn't have a lid, you can cover the sandwiches with a turned-over cast-iron skillet or Dutch oven.

7. Brush the tops of the sandwiches with butter and sprinkle each one with ½ to 1 teaspoon of the garlic powder and ½ to 1 tablespoon Parmesan cheese. Flip the sandwiches over and place them directly on the lower grill (if you were grilling on a top rack) over low heat. Brush the tops with butter and sprinkle with another ½ to 1 teaspoon garlic powder and ½ to 1 tablespoon Parmesan cheese. Cook until darker grill marks appear, 1 to 2 minutes, then flip and repeat on the opposite side. Serve.

I am with you always.

—Matthew 28:20

Beef Kebabs with Tangy Tequila Marinade

PREP TIME: 6 hours and 15 minutes

TOTAL TIME: 6 hours and 25 minutes

MAKES 4 SERVINGS

½ cup tequila

About ½ cup olive oil

3 tablespoons lime juice

3 tablespoons balsamic vinegar

3 tablespoons Worcestershire sauce

3 tablespoons light brown sugar

2 dried ancho chiles, crushed

2 (16-ounce) New York strip or sirloin steaks

8 to 10 white mushrooms

1 large white onion

3 or 4 jalapeños

2 yellow squash

4 to 6 sweet mini peppers, stemmed

Salt and black pepper

For great kebabs: Keep your meat and vegetables on separate skewers and cut them all roughly the same size. This marinade will help tenderize the steaks and also give a unique tang with its blend of balsamic vinegar, Worcestershire sauce, and tequila. The veggies blister for a good fired flavor. You can get creative with any kind you'd like to skewer up.

1. In a medium bowl, combine the tequila, 3 tablespoons of the olive oil, the lime juice, balsamic vinegar, Worcestershire sauce, brown sugar, and ancho chiles.

2. Cut the fat rind off the edges of the steaks and discard, then cut the meat into 1-inch chunks. Place the meat in a zippertop bag with the tequila marinade and refrigerate for at least 6 hours or overnight. Remove from the fridge about 20 minutes before grilling.

3. Stem the mushrooms and thread them onto their own skewers. (We prefer metal skewers because they won't burn while grilling.) Cut the remaining vegetables into 1-inch pieces and divide them among 5 or 6 skewers, alternating vegetables and leaving a little room between each piece.

4. Lightly pour 3 teaspoons of the olive oil over each of the vegetable skewers, then season with salt and pepper.

5. Thread the meat onto 4 or 5 skewers, leaving space between the pieces, and lightly season with salt and pepper.

6. Clean and oil the grill and move all the coals to one side. Preheat the grill. Grill the mushroom skewers on the low- or indirect-heat side of the grill until they begin to get tender,

4 to 5 minutes, then move them to the hotter side of the fire and grill, turning, until lightly charred, 2 to 3 minutes more.

7. Place the vegetable and meat skewers on the hot side of the grill. Cook the meat, turning the skewers occasionally, until it begins to sear, about 3 minutes, then move to lower heat and grill until medium rare, another 2 to 3 minutes. When the vegetables begin to blister, move them to the indirect-heat side of the fire and continue grilling, turning occasionally, until tender, about 3 minutes. Remove from the grill and let rest for a few minutes before serving.

Butter-Crusted Seared Pork Chops

PREP TIME: **6 hours and 5 minutes**
TOTAL TIME: **4 hours and 20 minutes**
MAKES 4 SERVINGS

2 tablespoons seasoned salt

2 tablespoons lemon pepper

1 tablespoon garlic powder

4 (1½-inch-thick) center-cut bone-in pork chops

Juice of 2 limes

Meat tenderizer

4 tablespoons clarified butter (see page 47) or peanut or canola oil

Creamy Dijon Sauce or Cherry-Bourbon Sauce (recipes follow)

OUTDOOR COOKING TIP

You can finish these chops in a Dutch oven with coals instead of using the oven. Place a heavy ring of hardwood coals around (not directly under) the bottom of a Dutch oven and a heavy layer on top. After about 3 minutes, flip the chops over and continue baking until the internal temperature is 145°F.

I do love me a big, thick bone-in pork chop. This is a great way to fix a chop to maximize the flavor and keep it juicy. We start off by searing the chops on the grill to seal in the moisture, and then finish them in the oven (or a Dutch oven) with some butter. Pork pairs well with fruits and sauces, so we're sharing a Creamy Dijon Sauce and a Cherry-Bourbon Sauce to enhance its flavor.

———— ❖ ————

1. In a small bowl, combine the seasoned salt, lemon pepper, and garlic powder.

2. Rub both sides of the chops with the lime juice. Sprinkle both sides with the meat tenderizer, followed by the seasoning mix, and rub in well. Cover and refrigerate for 4 hours.

3. Meanwhile, preheat the oven to 400°F and heat a large cast-iron skillet in the oven for 20 minutes before grilling.

4. Clean, oil, and preheat the grill. Grill the chops over a hot fire for about 2 minutes per side, until they just begin to char.

5. Remove the skillet from the oven and add the butter. When the butter has melted, add the chops and flip them to coat both sides.

6. Return the skillet to the oven and bake for 8 to 10 minutes, turning the chops over about halfway through baking, until the internal temperature is 145°F. Let the chops rest for a couple of minutes before serving. Top with one of the sauces, if desired.

PREP TIME: 2 minutes
TOTAL TIME: 5 minutes
MAKES ABOUT 1½ CUPS

1 cup heavy cream
½ cup chicken broth
2 tablespoons butter, melted
Leaves from 2 sprigs fresh thyme, minced
2 tablespoons Dijon mustard

Creamy Dijon Sauce

In a small saucepan, whisk together all the ingredients over medium-high heat. Bring to a heavy rapid simmer, stirring constantly, for about 2 minutes, until heated through. Serve.

PREP TIME: 2 minutes
TOTAL TIME: 5 minutes
MAKES ABOUT 1 CUP

½ cup cherry preserves
¼ cup light brown sugar
¼ cup whiskey or bourbon
2 tablespoons olive oil

Cherry-Bourbon Sauce

In a small saucepan, whisk together all the ingredients over medium heat. Bring to a simmer, stirring frequently, for about 2 minutes, until heated through. Serve warm.

Hats and cowboys both require shaping—one by man, the other by God.

Sage-and-Pear Pork Loin

PREP TIME: **4 hours and 15 minutes**

TOTAL TIME: **4 hours and 55 minutes**

MAKES ABOUT 6 SERVINGS

1 (6- to 6½-pound) whole pork loin

Lime juice

Meat tenderizer

Salt and black pepper

3 Granny Smith apples, peeled and cored

2 Bartlett pears, peeled and cored

½ stick butter, melted

2 tablespoons light brown sugar

3 tablespoons finely chopped fresh sage leaves

2 to 3 teaspoons ground cinnamon

2 to 3 teaspoons ground nutmeg

1 to 2 cups apple-cherry juice or other fruit juice for spraying

A pork loin is a great cut because it will serve several folks and isn't going to empty your wallet. We butterfly the loin, roll it out, and stuff it with pears, apples, fresh sage, and a little nutmeg and cinnamon for spice. We call this our holiday loin, because it has some classic fall flavors and can be served at Thanksgiving instead of turkey. But you don't need a special occasion as a reason to serve this up—just some special folks you love.

---

1. Butterfly the pork loin (see Tip). Rub a generous amount of lime juice on both sides of the loin, then sprinkle both sides with meat tenderizer, salt, and pepper to taste and rub in. Cover and refrigerate for about 4 hours. About 20 minutes before grilling, remove from the fridge.

2. Meanwhile, thinly slice the apples and pears. Place them in a medium saucepan with the butter, then stir in the brown sugar. Cook over medium heat, stirring occasionally, until the fruit begins to soften, about 8 minutes.

3. With a slotted spoon, remove the fruit from the saucepan and spread it lengthwise down the middle of the loin. Drizzle with about 2 tablespoons of the butter from the pan. Sprinkle the sage on top, followed by the cinnamon and nutmeg to taste.

4. Begin on a long side of the loin and tightly roll it up. Tightly tie one end with butcher's string. Proceed to use a half-hitch knot to tie up the loin and tie it off at the end. You can also cut the string in short sections and tie it around the loin every couple of inches to secure it.

(recipe continues)

TIP

To butterfly the pork loin,
hold your knife parallel to the
cutting board about a third of
the way from the bottom of the
meat and make a horizontal
slice lengthwise through the
loin, stopping about 1 inch from
the end; do not cut all the way
through. Unroll the flap. Make
another horizontal cut into the
thicker side of the loin, again
stopping about 1 inch from the
end, and unroll. You can also
ask your butcher to do this.

5. Clean and oil the grill and move all the coals to one side. Preheat the grill to medium. Place the loin on the indirect-heat side of the grill. Add the apple-cherry juice to a spray bottle and spray the loin generously. Close the lid and cook for 15 minutes.

6. Open the lid and flip the loin over. Generously spray with the juice, close the lid, and cook for another 15 minutes.

7. Rake the coals so they are evenly distributed and move the loin over direct heat. Turn the loin and spray generously with the juice. Shut the lid and grill for 5 minutes.

8. Keep the lid open and continue grilling, turning the loin a quarter turn every few minutes and basting frequently with the juice, until it is an evenly browned and lightly charred color and the internal temperature is 145°F, about 5 minutes. Let the loin rest for a few minutes, then cut into 1-inch-thick slices and serve.

Fall-Apart Ribs

PREP TIME: **4 hours**
TOTAL TIME: **6 hours and 45 minutes**
MAKES 6 TO 8 SERVINGS

2 tablespoons seasoned salt

2 tablespoons lemon pepper

2 tablespoons crushed dried ancho chile

2 tablespoons smoked paprika

1 tablespoon garlic powder

2 (2 to 3 pounds) racks baby back ribs

Juice of 2 limes

4 tablespoons meat tenderizer

1 (32-ounce) carton chicken broth

Good ribs need to be tender and have great flavor. The secret is steaming them first. We steam them with chicken broth, which you can do on the grill or in the oven. After they have cooked nearly through, you throw them on the fire to give them a good smokiness that complements the meat well.

————•‑•————

1. In a small bowl, combine the seasoned salt, lemon pepper, crushed ancho chile, smoked paprika, and garlic powder.

2. Beginning at the smaller end of the ribs, and using a paper towel, peel back the membrane from the bone side of the ribs. (The paper towel will give you a better grip.) Chilling the ribs in the freezer for 10 minutes will also make for easier membrane removal.

3. Rub the lime juice on both sides of the ribs. Sprinkle about 1 tablespoon meat tenderizer on each side of both racks of ribs and the seasoning blend on the meat side and rub in well. Cover and refrigerate for about 4 hours or overnight. Remove the racks from the refrigerator about 30 minutes before cooking.

4. Preheat the oven to 300°F.

5. Place the ribs in a Dutch oven or large foil pan, bone side down. (You may need to cut the ribs to fit in your cooking vessel.) Pour in about 2 inches of chicken broth. Cover with the lid or foil and cook for 2 to 2½ hours, until fork-tender.

6. Meanwhile, clean, oil, and preheat the grill to medium-high. Remove the ribs from the oven and place them on the grill. Grill, turning occasionally and basting with the excess chicken broth, until they are dark golden brown and the meat begins to pull away from the bone, about 6 to 8 minutes.

OUTDOOR COOKING TIP

Instead of cooking in a conventional oven, you can start the ribs in a Dutch oven. Arrange a generous amount of hardwood or hardwood lump charcoal coals in a ring around (not directly under) the bottom of the Dutch oven and spread a solid layer on the lid. You will need to add more chicken broth as the ribs cook. Baste every 15 minutes.

Grilled Shrimp in Chipotle-Honey Marinade

PREP TIME: **6 hours and 15 minutes**

TOTAL TIME: **6 hours and 30 minutes**

MAKES 4 TO 6 SERVINGS

6 tablespoons olive oil

3 tablespoons honey

Juice of 1 lime

4 garlic cloves, minced

3 chipotle chiles in adobo sauce, finely chopped

1 teaspoon sea salt

1 teaspoon coarsely ground black pepper

½ teaspoon ground cumin

20 to 25 large shrimp, peeled and deveined

This marinade is the perfect blend of heat and sweet. Chipotle chiles are one of my favorite ingredients because they have a smoky kick to them. The honey mellows the heat a bit, and cumin and garlic add even more flavor for your tastebuds to enjoy. After the shrimp take a good bath in the marinade, they are lightly kissed by fire and smoke. This can be served as a main course or an appetizer. The marinade also works well with chicken.

1. In a medium bowl, whisk together the olive oil, honey, lime juice, garlic, chipotles, salt, pepper, and cumin.

2. Remove the tails from the shrimp and discard. Toss the shrimp in the marinade until well coated. Transfer to a zippertop bag and refrigerate for at least 6 hours or overnight.

3. Remove the shrimp from the bag and thread them onto grilling skewers (we prefer metal ones), 4 to 5 shrimp per skewer.

4. Clean, oil, and preheat the grill to low. Move the coals to one side of the grill and grill the skewers over indirect heat for 2 to 3 minutes per side.

5. Move the skewers to the hotter side of the grill and cook for 1½ to 2 minutes per side, until opaque. Let cool slightly before serving.

Smoky Asian Grilled Salmon

PREP TIME: **15 minutes**
TOTAL TIME: **20 minutes**
MAKES 4 SERVINGS

1 (1- to 2-pound) side of salmon or 4 (4-ounce) fillets

1 tablespoon coarse sea salt

1 to 2 tablespoons coarsely ground black pepper

3 tablespoons butter, melted

1 tablespoon olive or avocado oil

1 garlic clove, minced

3 tablespoons light brown sugar

1 teaspoon soy sauce

1 teaspoon paprika or smoked paprika

Juice of 1 lemon

Grilling fish can be a little intimidating, because it sometimes wants to stick to the grill. Using coarse sea salt on the skin side of salmon helps prevent sticking. Also, be sure to start with a well-oiled grill and oil your spatula before flipping it. We baste the fish with a smoky Asian-style sauce with a little soy sauce and brown sugar for sweetness.

———◆◆◆———

1. Season both sides of the salmon with about ½ tablespoon salt and press in lightly. Season the meat side of the salmon with the pepper. Let sit for 10 minutes.

2. Meanwhile, in a small saucepan, whisk together the butter, oil, garlic, and brown sugar. Cook over medium heat, stirring occasionally, until it begins to warm. Stir in the soy sauce, paprika, and lemon juice and continue cooking, stirring occasionally, until the sauce reaches a low boil, about 3 minutes. Remove from the heat and set aside.

3. Clean, oil, and preheat the grill to medium-high. Place the salmon flesh side down on the grill, close the lid, and cook for 2 to 2½ minutes (for a fillet that is 1 inch thick or less), until the skin just begins to turn white around the edges. Flip and cook for another 1½ to 2 minutes, with the lid open, just until the fish is flaky.

4. Baste the flesh side of the fish with the sauce, close the lid, and cook for 1 minute. Baste the flesh side again and cook for 30 seconds with the lid open. Remove from the grill and let rest for a few minutes. Baste again before serving.

Asparagus with Parmesan Cream Sauce

PREP TIME: **15 minutes**
TOTAL TIME: **25 minutes**
MAKES ABOUT 6 SERVINGS

½ stick butter

¾ cup heavy cream

1 large egg

Juice of ½ lemon

3 to 4 tablespoons grated Parmesan cheese

Coarse sea salt

Coarsely ground black pepper

2 pounds asparagus, ends trimmed

Olive oil

Asparagus is best on the grill, which gives it flavor and also makes it more tender. We start it off with just a little olive oil, salt, and black pepper. The grand finale is the sauce we drizzle on top before serving. It's a soft blend of cream, lemon, and Parmesan cheese.

—◆—

1. Melt the butter in a medium saucepan over medium heat on the grill or stovetop. Stir in the cream and simmer for a few minutes, stirring frequently, until warmed through.

2. Beat the egg in a small bowl and slowly whisk in the lemon juice. Slowly add the egg mixture to the warm cream, whisking constantly until it thickens just slightly, about 4 minutes. Stir in the Parmesan cheese to taste. Season with salt and pepper to taste. Keep warm.

3. In a baking dish, toss the asparagus with enough olive oil to generously coat. Sprinkle with salt and pepper to taste. Cover and let sit for 10 minutes.

4. Meanwhile, clean, oil, and preheat the grill to medium-high. Place the asparagus on the grill, close the lid, and grill, turning frequently, until tender and lightly charred, about 3 to 4 minutes. Serve warm, topped with the Parmesan cream sauce.

Mexican Street Corn on the Cob

PREP TIME: 10 minutes
TOTAL TIME: 20 minutes
MAKES 6 SERVINGS

3 tablespoons sour cream

3 tablespoons mayonnaise

2 tablespoons grated Parmesan cheese, plus more for sprinkling

1 tablespoon lime juice

½ teaspoon chili powder

½ teaspoon garlic powder

½ teaspoon ground cumin

¼ teaspoon ancho chile powder

6 ears sweet corn, shucked

Olive oil

Salt and black pepper

I have shucked many an ear of corn in my lifetime, and my favorite way to eat it is grilled. The smoke and char create another layer of flavor, but the star of this show is the spread, which you'll want to generously slather all over the corn. The creamy mix of sour cream and mayonnaise is spiced up with cumin, chili powder, garlic, and Parmesan cheese. The spread also makes a great dip for chips.

1. In a small bowl, whisk together the sour cream, mayonnaise, Parmesan cheese, lime juice, chili powder, garlic powder, cumin, and ancho chile powder.

2. Rub the corn with olive oil, then sprinkle with salt and pepper to taste.

3. Clean, oil, and preheat the grill to medium-high. Place the corn on the grill, close the lid, and cook, turning frequently, until lightly charred and softened, about 10 minutes.

4. Remove the corn from the grill and let cool slightly. Generously brush with the sour cream mixture, sprinkle with more Parmesan, and serve immediately.

If you go through life thinking you don't get a fair shake, try reaching out and shaking more hands and making more friends.

Grilled Romaine with Honey Vinaigrette

PREP TIME: **10 minutes**
TOTAL TIME: **15 minutes**
MAKES 6 SERVINGS

¼ cup olive oil

1 tablespoon lime juice

¼ teaspoon ancho chile powder

Salt and black pepper

3 hearts of romaine lettuce, halved lengthwise

Crumbled bacon or bacon bits for topping (optional)

Honey Vinaigrette (opposite)

I'm a beef guy. I've raised it, fed it, cooked it, and cussed it when it was trying to run me over in the pasture. So naturally, when I first started cooking I thought the grill was only for meat, but boy, was I wrong. Romaine is my favorite type of lettuce, and it's perfect for the grill, because its hardier stalks hold up well on the heat. We top the salad with a homemade vinaigrette with a little honey, hot sauce, and balsamic vinegar.

—◆—

1. In a small bowl, whisk together the olive oil, lime juice, chile powder, and salt and pepper to taste. Generously baste the cut side of each romaine half with the mixture.

2. Clean, oil, and preheat the grill to medium-high. Grill the romaine cut side down just until the leaves wilt slightly and a char appears, 2 to 3 minutes.

3. Generously baste the tops of the romaine halves with the olive oil mixture, flip them over, and grill until slightly charred, 2 to 3 minutes more.

4. Remove from the grill, top with the bacon (if using) and drizzle with the vinaigrette. Serve.

Honey Vinaigrette

PREP TIME: 2 minutes
TOTAL TIME: 2 minutes
MAKES ABOUT 1 CUP

½ cup mayonnaise

¼ cup honey

2 tablespoons balsamic vinegar

4 teaspoons hot sauce

½ teaspoon smoked paprika

½ teaspoon salt or sea salt

½ teaspoon coarsely ground black pepper

Mix all the ingredients together in a small bowl. Serve immediately over grilled romaine, or cover and chill until ready to serve.

A feller asked me once, "Do you serve three-course meals?" I replied, "Yep, anticipation, satisfaction, and a recliner!"

Chocolate–Peanut Butter Grilled Banana Splits

PREP TIME: **15 minutes**
TOTAL TIME: **25 minutes**
MAKES 4 SERVINGS

4 bananas

1 cup semisweet or milk chocolate chips

1 cup peanut butter chips

4 to 8 tablespooons sweetened condensed milk

Finely chopped pecans, ice cream, or whipped cream for serving (optional)

Let's throw some fruit on the grill for an ooey-gooey treat. This is a great summer dessert and fun to cook up with the kids. The bananas are grilled in their skins just long enough to get them softened. We then fill them with chocolate and peanut butter chips until they melt and top them with sweetened condensed milk for extra richness. This is an easy pleaser.

———◆◆◆———

1. Clean, oil, and preheat the grill to high. Grill the unpeeled bananas, rotating frequently, until the skins begin to turn dark and the bananas soften slightly, 3 to 5 minutes.

2. Remove the bananas from the grill and slice them lengthwise down the center, being careful not to cut completely through them. Using your fingers or a spoon, lightly spread the bananas apart to create a trough in the middle.

3. Fill the middle of each banana with a layer of chocolate chips, followed by the peanut butter chips.

4. Place the bananas back on the grill over low heat and close the lid. Grill just until the chips begin to soften, 3 to 5 minutes. Spoon 1 to 2 tablespoons of the condensed milk down the middle of each banana, then close the grill and cook until the milk has warmed through, about 3 minutes. Remove from the grill and serve immediately, still in the peels, topped with nuts, ice cream, or whipped cream, if desired.

Jacked-Up Peaches

PREP TIME: **5 minutes**
TOTAL TIME: **15 minutes**
MAKES 6 SERVINGS

3 peaches
½ stick butter
⅓ cup honey
2 tablespoons Jack Daniel's whiskey (or other whiskey)
2 teaspoons ground cinnamon
Ice cream or whipped cream for serving

It's peach-picking time, and you better pick a few extra! When you grill a sweet fruit, you maximize the sugar and get great caramelization. Baste these rascals with Jack Daniel's whiskey, honey, and a dash of cinnamon to really make the peach flavor pop. We top them off with ice cream or whipped cream for a perfect summer dessert.

————◆◆————

1. Cut the peaches in half, remove the pits, and slightly hollow them out to hold the ice cream or whipped cream after grilling.

2. Melt the butter in a small saucepan over medium heat. Whisk in the honey, whiskey, and cinnamon and cook, whisking constantly, until warmed through, about 3 minutes.

3. Clean, oil, and preheat the grill to medium-high. Grill the peaches skin side down for 2 to 3 minutes, until they begin to char slightly.

4. Baste the hollowed-out side of the peaches with the honey glaze and flip them over. Grill for another 3 to 4 minutes, until tender and slightly charred, lifting the peaches and basting the hollowed-out side at least twice while they cook.

5. Remove the peaches from the grill and place a scoop of ice cream or whipped cream in the hollowed-out side. Drizzle with a little leftover honey glaze and serve.

Pasture and Pond

Beef, Pork, Fins, and Feathers

As the cowboys rode out, part of me wished I was back in the saddle again. It was a beautiful spring morning in the Palo Duro Canyon in the Texas Panhandle, so instead of washing dishes, I took a seat and watched as they rode out of sight. I knew they were doing what they loved, and it was the same for me. I had been where they were, so I knew what their day might consist of. It could entail mounting a horse that wanted to buck you off first thing in the morning or trying to rope an ol' cow that had other plans.

My day, though, probably wouldn't be that challenging. That is, unless Mother Nature decided to bring me a forty-five-mph breeze or snowstorm right when I'm trying to finish supper, which she has done on occasion. But I did miss those big pastures—some as large as 3,500 acres. The view between a horse's ears, looking out on the vast countryside scattered with mesquite, cactus, and sage, is humbling. To be on horse-back on top of a rocky canyon rim, looking at cattle below as they weave their way through the ravines and catching a glimpse of a lone cowboy in pursuit of the bovines, was always breathtaking. This is God's country and as close to heaven as we may get here on earth.

It makes a man's heart full to be a part of a big pasture. We sure don't take things for granted out here. We're always thankful for the smallest drop of rain or a newborn baby calf. It's the little things in life that often are the most rewarding.

I think of all the folks I've fed as a chuck-wagon cook, the wood I've burned, and the many dishes I've washed. It's never been a job but more of a reward. I learned a long time ago that success comes from the heart, not the wallet. It's about having purpose, having faith, and not being afraid to follow your dreams and take steps into bigger pastures.

I don't care where you live or what you do, whether your pasture is made up of red dirt, green grass, concrete, or asphalt, success is about enjoying the pasture where you are and the folks you get to share it with.

The Perfect 10-Minute Beef Filet

PREP TIME: **2 hours**

TOTAL TIME: **2 hours and 15 minutes**

MAKES 2 SERVINGS

2 (6-ounce) filets mignons

Coarse sea salt

Coarsely ground black pepper

Melted clarified butter (see page 47) or peanut or canola oil

1 tablespoon butter

To cook a steak past medium rare is like having a root canal. Both of them make it hard to chew!

If you've wondered how to sear a beef filet so it's cooked perfectly, here's a recipe for you. The filet mignon, also known as the tenderloin, is the most tender cut of beef, as its name suggests. Add a light layer of oil or clarified butter to a hot cast-iron skillet and then get to searing! This is a timed event, folks, so get the stopwatch out to evenly sear the sides. The steak finishes in the oven to a juicy rare to medium rare.

———◆◆———

1. Generously rub the filets with salt and pepper, making sure to season all sides and edges. Put them in a zippertop bag and refrigerate for 2 hours. Remove from the fridge about 40 minutes before cooking.

2. Meanwhile, preheat the oven to 450°F.

3. Heat a large cast-iron skillet over high heat for 2 minutes. Pour in just enough clarified butter to lightly coat the bottom.

4. Place the filets in the skillet and cook for 2 minutes. Flip and cook for another 2 minutes. Set the filets on edge and cook the four edges for 1 minute each, for a total of 4 minutes.

5. Place the first side that you seared down in the skillet. Top the filets with ½ tablespoon butter each, transfer to the oven, and roast for 2 minutes. For medium-rare meat, cook for another 1½ to 2 minutes.

6. Remove the filets from the skillet and let rest on a cutting board for 3 to 5 minutes. Serve warm.

Slow-Cooker Pot Roast

PREP TIME: **3 hours and 15 minutes**

TOTAL TIME: **8 hours and 15 minutes**

MAKES 6 TO 8 SERVINGS

2 tablespoons coarsely ground black pepper

1 tablespoon seasoned salt

1 tablespoon paprika or smoked paprika

1 teaspoon garlic powder

1 teaspoon celery salt

1 teaspoon ground thyme

Lime juice

1 (3½- to 4-pound) chuck roast

6 garlic cloves, peeled

2 cups beef broth

2 bay leaves, crumbled

2 tablespoons vegetable oil

3 russet potatoes, quartered

6 to 8 carrots, peeled, halved lengthwise, then cut into 2-inch pieces

2 yellow onions, sliced into large chunks

1 dried guajillo chile, stemmed, seeded, and chopped

Before letting the slow cooker do all the work, I like to sear the meat, which locks in flavor. A little thyme, celery salt, and whole garlic cloves season the meat nicely. Instead of a chuck roast, you can also use an arm, bottom round, or neck roast. I also like to save the broth and mix it with some cornstarch and water to thicken, then add a little cream to make a gravy to pour on top.

---

1. In a small bowl, combine the pepper, seasoned salt, paprika, garlic powder, celery salt, and thyme.

2. Rub lime juice on all sides of the roast. Generously sprinkle with the seasoning blend and rub to coat all sides. With a knife, poke 6 small holes evenly around the roast and push the garlic cloves into them. Cover and refrigerate for 3 hours. Remove from the fridge about 30 minutes before cooking.

3. Meanwhile, turn the slow cooker to high and add the beef broth and bay leaves.

4. Heat the oil in a large cast-iron skillet over high heat. Sear the roast for about 3 minutes per side and 1 to 2 minutes on the edges.

5. Place the roast in the slow cooker. Add the potatoes, carrots, onions, and chile and season with any leftover seasoning blend, to taste. Cover with the lid and cook for about 5 hours, or until the veggies are done and the meat is tender enough to pull apart with a fork. Slice and serve.

Prize-Winning Cowboy Chili

PREP TIME: 15 minutes

TOTAL TIME: 55 minutes

MAKES 6 TO 8 SERVINGS

2 pounds ground beef or chuck, cut into bite-sized chunks

Salt and black pepper

1 large yellow onion, chopped

2 (10-ounce) cans Ro-Tel diced tomatoes and green chiles, drained

1 (15-ounce) can tomato sauce

1 (16-ounce) can kidney beans, drained

3 or 4 chipotle chiles in adobo sauce, chopped

⅓ cup chili powder

1 tablespoon minced garlic

2 teaspoons dried oregano

2 teaspoons paprika or smoked paprika

½ teaspoon ground cumin

Shredded cheddar cheese, sour cream, and chopped green onions for serving

So, here's the funny thing—we've never actually won any prizes ourselves with this recipe. However, we've gotten a ton of emails from folks who tell us they used this recipe at their local chili cook-off and won! You can use any type of meat, whether it's ground beef or even wild game. A perfect blend of chili powder, cumin, and oregano gives it a classic chili flavor, and the chipotle chiles take it to blue ribbon status! Beans or no beans is always the question. I do love a bean, and we add kidney beans for more heartiness, but that's your call.

---

1. In a large pot or 12-inch Dutch oven, brown the meat over medium-high heat, breaking up the chopped beef or turning the cubes of chuck, 8 to 10 minutes. As the meat begins to brown, season with salt and pepper to taste. Stir in the onion and continue cooking until the meat has fully browned and the onion is tender, 3 to 5 minutes. Drain the excess grease.

2. Stir in the Ro-Tel tomatoes and chiles, 1 Ro-Tel can of water, the tomato sauce, kidney beans, and chipotle chiles to taste. Stir in 2 teaspoons salt and the remaining seasonings.

3. Cover and bring to a boil for 5 minutes. Reduce the heat and simmer, stirring occasionally, for about 40 minutes, to let the flavors blend. Serve warm, topped with cheese, sour cream, and green onions, if desired.

CAST-IRON TIP

Acidic foods, such as tomatoes or barbecue sauces, are harsh on cast iron, but you can cook them in it. Just be sure to clean it well and reseason it after every use.

Catch a Rabbit

Blessings come in all forms and in packages big and small. About three years ago, we got one of those blessings.

He just showed up in the yard one day, bearing gifts. First there was an old chewed-up boot, then a stuffed teddy bear with one arm, and after that, several gloves. None of them matched, of course. He was a speckled bird dog, and he was a character. He was the happiest dog I have ever been around in my life, and I have been around a lot of happy dogs.

We saw him often, but he would come and go. For a long time, he wouldn't get in our pickup, but he would follow us all over town. He knew the fastest route to the grocery store, post office, and any high school sporting event. Folks would ask, "Is that y'all's dog waiting at the door?" I would just smile and say, "He sure thinks so."

One day, he figured out our dog door, and when we arrived home from running errands, there was our blessing stretched out fast asleep on the couch like he owned the place. From that point on, we claimed him full time. We called him Frank the Wonder Dog because we always wondered what he was getting into and what he was thinking.

He still showered us with gifts, I suppose to show his gratitude. After we'd been away on a cooking tour and arrived home, the yard would be sprinkled with Tupperware and mismatched shoes. It would always be the right shoe, because for some reason he never picked up a left one. The best gift we ever got from him was a turtle. We're still really not sure how he got the whole thing in his mouth or where it came from. The gifts weren't anything special, but they were special to Frank, because I think he methodically chose each one to bring back to us.

This dog showed us a lot about life. Every day was a holiday to him, and he made the most out of each one. He was always the first one to greet me every morning. He made me smile as he stretched and let out a little grumble as if to say, "It's about time you got up, Dad, we are missing out on a great day to catch something!"

We witnessed Frank's never-give-up attitude every day. You see, there was a cottontail rabbit that lived under the deck in the backyard. Frank and this rabbit played many hours of "catch me if you can." Frank would stand on the deck and bark for hours as if he thought he might lure the little feller out. He would creep through the yard with each step so soft as if not to make a sound on the grass. Every time I would tell him, "Frank, you ain't going to catch that rabbit." But it didn't matter to Frank. He loved the hunt, and he loved the adventure.

Frank became quite the star on our YouTube channel. His carefree attitude was contagious. He had a knack for coming on camera just long enough to hike a leg and wet something down. He made folks laugh. And as he stuck his head out the window of the pickup to feel the wind against his face, he made us thankful for another great adventure each day.

Tragically, we lost Frank one morning. He wasn't just a dog, he was family. I dug a hole right by the deck where he had lain for so many hours waiting on that rabbit. I filled that hole with tears and with the happiest dog I have ever known.

The next morning long before sunrise, I poured myself a cup of coffee and sat by Frank's grave, wondering how I would make it without my friend. As the sun began to peek through the darkness, I noticed something moving in the grass on the other side of the yard. It was Frank's buddy, the rabbit. He didn't move and neither did I. It was like he was standing at attention paying tribute to a fallen comrade. I sat there silent for what seemed like hours, hoping to hear Frank bark to sound the alarm.

And then I heard it as plain as day: "Catch a rabbit." At that moment, the tears ran down my face like rain. I realized I can't give up or be afraid to take a chance, or stop doing what's in my heart because someone doesn't think I can.

Many sunsets have come and gone since that day. Still, every time I open the back gate, I think of Frank sneaking around the corner, just knowing he was going to catch that rabbit. It still brings a tear now and then, but the memories of our comical dog and his never-give-up spirit have eased the pain.

There will be days in life when you feel like you're coming up short or that you just can't do it anymore. But when those feelings creep in, just remember Frank the Wonder Dog, who always had hope and was always thankful for the littlest blessings in life. Now, go catch a rabbit!

Enchiladas with Homemade Red Sauce

PREP TIME: **35minutes**

TOTAL TIME: **1 hour and 5 minutes**

MAKES ABOUT 6 SERVINGS;
MAKES ABOUT 4 CUPS SAUCE

1 pound ground beef

1 yellow onion, chopped

1 (4-ounce) can chopped green chiles

Salt and black pepper

12 dried guajillo chiles, stemmed and seeded

3 teaspoons minced garlic

3 (8-ounce) cans tomato sauce

2 teaspoons ancho chile powder

1½ teaspoons chili powder

1 teaspoon ground cumin

⅓ cup chicken broth

12 corn tortillas

3 cups shredded cheddar cheese

1 cup shredded mozzarella cheese

Folks, I know it's easy to grab a can of enchilada sauce from the grocery store. Hey, I've used it in a lot of recipes. But if you want that truly special homemade flavor, you need to make this sauce. A bold blend of dried chiles, onion, garlic, and traditional Mexican spices cooks up into a red sauce. This isn't like that runny out-of-the-can sauce; this is thick and hearty! Pour it over corn tortillas filled with seasoned ground beef and, of course, lots of cheese!

1. In a medium cast-iron skillet, begin browning the meat over medium-high heat, stirring to break it up. When it begins to brown, stir in half the onion and the green chiles; season with salt and pepper to taste. Continue cooking until the meat has browned and the onion is tender, 5 minutes.

2. Meanwhile, make the enchilada sauce. Add the guajillo chiles, the remaining onion, and 1 teaspoon of the minced garlic to a medium saucepan. Cover with water and bring to a boil until the peppers soften, about 20 minutes.

3. Preheat the oven to 350°F.

4. Strain the chiles, onion, and garlic from the pan (discard the liquid) and place in a blender. Add the tomato sauce, the remaining 2 teaspoons garlic, the ancho chile powder, chili powder, and cumin. Blend until smooth and then season with salt and pepper to taste. Strain the mixture back into the saucepan.

5. Stir in the chicken broth, and simmer on medium-low heat for 2 minutes, stirring occasionally.

OUTDOOR COOKING TIP

When cooking in a Dutch oven with hardwood coals, after the enchiladas begin to lightly bubble (before you've topped them with the cheese), move back or reduce the coals around the bottom so as not to burn the sauce.

6. Spread a light layer of the enchilada sauce in a 12-inch cast-iron skillet or 9-x-13-inch casserole dish.

7. Place a tortilla on a work surface and spoon 2 to 3 table-spoons of the meat mixture evenly down the middle. Top with about 1 tablespoon of the cheddar cheese and roll up tightly. Place in the skillet or casserole dish seam side down and repeat with the remaining tortillas, meat, and cheddar. Pour the remaining sauce over the enchiladas.

8. Bake for about 25 minutes, or until the tortillas soften. Sprinkle the remaining cheddar and the mozzarella on top, return to the oven, and bake for another 5 minutes, or until the cheese has melted.

Chicken, Ham, and Cheese Roll-Up

PREP TIME: **1 hour and 20 minutes**
TOTAL TIME: **1 hour and 50 minutes**
MAKES **6 TO 8 SERVINGS**

Braided Onion French Bread (116)

2 tablespoons butter

2 tablespoons all-purpose flour, plus more for dusting

1 cup milk

2 tablespoons Dijon mustard, plus more for serving (optional)

1 tablespoon lemon juice

8 to 10 ounces sliced deli chicken

8 to 10 ounces sliced deli ham

8 ounces sliced provolone cheese

1 large egg white

1 tablespoon water

I like to think of this as a big, grown-up-style Hot Pocket. Shan has taken her Braided French Onion Bread and topped it with sliced chicken, ham, and cheese and a creamy Dijon sauce. Then she rolls it up and bakes it for a gooey dish that has homemade bread flavor.

1. Follow steps 1 through 4 of the recipe for Braided Onion French Bread.

2. While the dough is rising, melt the butter in a small saucepan over medium heat. Whisk in the flour and milk and cook, whisking frequently, until the mixture thickens to a gravy consistency, about 3 minutes. Stir in the Dijon mustard and lemon juice. Set aside.

3. Preheat the oven to 375°F with a rack in the middle. Butter a baking sheet.

4. After the dough has risen, turn it out onto a floured surface and knead slightly, adding more flour to remove any stickiness. The dough is easier to roll up if it's not too moist. Roll out into a 15-x-11-inch rectangle.

5. Place a layer of the chicken on the dough, followed by the ham and provolone cheese. Whisk the Dijon sauce and evenly spread it on the cheese.

6. Starting with a long side of the dough, roll it up as tightly as possible. Tuck the ends under. Place the roll, seam side down, on the baking sheet.

7. In a small bowl, whisk together the egg white and water. Brush the roll with the egg wash and top with the poppy seed mixture from the Braided Onion French Bread recipe.

8. Bake for 25 to 30 minutes, until golden brown on the top and bottom . Let cool for 5 minutes before cutting into 1-inch-thick slices. Serve with Dijon mustard, if desired.

Crispy Chiles Rellenos

PREP TIME: **30 minutes**
TOTAL TIME: **45 minutes**
MAKES 4 TO 6 SERVINGS

1 pound ground beef
(80% lean)

½ yellow onion, chopped

2 garlic cloves, minced

2 teaspoons chili powder

1 teaspoon dried oregano

3 tablespoons cornstarch

1½ teaspoons ground cumin

1½ teaspoons baking powder

1½ teaspoons salt

1½ teaspoons black pepper

1½ cups all-purpose flour

1½ (12-ounce) cans light beer

4 to 6 large poblano chiles,
roasted (see Tip on page 227)
and gently peeled

1 to 1½ cups shredded
Monterey Jack cheese, plus
more for sprinkling

Peanut or canola oil for frying

Our chiles rellenos start with chile peppers stuffed with ground beef, cheese, and spices; these are then dipped in a beer batter and deep-fried. We use poblano chiles because of their natural smokiness, and we roast them before stuffing to bring out their flavor. For a crust with the perfect crispness, we add light beer and cornstarch to the batter.

———— ••• ————

1. Cook the beef in a medium skillet over medium-high heat, stirring to break it up. When it begins to brown, stir in the onion, garlic, chili powder, and oregano. Continue cooking until the beef has browned and the onion is tender, 8 to 10 minutes. Set aside.

2. In a wide bowl, whisk together the cornstarch, cumin, baking powder, salt, pepper, and flour. Slowly pour in the beer until it reaches the consistency of pancake batter.

3. Cut a slit down the middle of the poblanos from the top, leaving ½ to 1 inch from the bottom uncut. Carefully remove the seeds with a spoon. Sprinkle about ¼ cup of cheese in each pepper, followed by about 2 tablespoons beef, depending on the size of the peppers. Use wooden grilling skewers or toothpicks to hold the seams together.

4. Pour in enough oil to reach about halfway up the side of a large cast-iron skillet. Heat to 350°F over medium-high heat.

5. Add the stuffed peppers to the batter and spoon the mixture over to evenly coat. Be sure to cover the open seams of the peppers with batter so they will seal when frying. Place a few of the peppers at a time in the oil, uncut side down,

and fry until golden brown, 1 to 2 minutes. Using tongs, carefully flip the peppers and fry them seam side down until golden brown, another 1 to 2 minutes. Remove from the oil with tongs and let cool slightly on a paper towel or wire rack. Top with more cheese, if desired. Remove the toothpicks before serving. Serve hot.

Indian Tacos

PREP TIME: **2 hours and 30 minutes**

TOTAL TIME: **2 hours and 45 minutes**

MAKES 10 TACOS

Indian Fry Bread (page 259)

Ranch Refried Beans (page 143) or 2 (15-ounce) cans pinto beans, drained

1 pound ground beef

Salt and black pepper

Shredded cheddar cheese, diced onions, chopped tomatoes, shredded lettuce, and sour cream for topping

If y'all haven't had this staple of local and state fairs, don't worry, because we've brought the fair to you! Start off by using our Indian Fry Bread recipe, a soft, rich dough fried up golden brown. From there, you can get creative and top it off however you like, but we suggest our spiced-up pinto beans and ground beef, finished with cheese, onions, tomatoes, and lettuce . . . just to name a few possibilities.

---

1. Follow step 1 of the recipe for Indian Fry Bread.

2. While the dough is resting, follow steps 1 and 2 of the Ranch Refried Beans recipe, boiling the beans until tender. Drain the water and return the beans to the pot they were cooked in. For high elevation cooking, use canned beans.

3. Meanwhile, in a medium skillet, brown the beef over medium-high heat. Season with salt and pepper to taste.

4. Shape and fry the bread as directed in steps 2 and 3 of the Indian Fry Bread recipe.

5. Stir the beef into the beans, spoon the mixture onto the fry breads, and serve immediately, topped with shredded cheese, onions, tomatoes, lettuce, and sour cream.

As Mama always said, "There are two ways to get iron in your system—that's eating out of it, or by me hitting you with it when you don't mind your manners!"

Foolproof Prime Rib

PREP TIME: **2 hours and 10 minutes**

TOTAL TIME: **4 hours and 40 minutes**

MAKES 6 SERVINGS

1 (5- to 6-pound) bone-in rib roast (prime rib)

1 stick butter, softened

1 tablespoon olive oil

2 tablespoons coarsely ground black pepper

2 tablespoons coarse sea salt, plus more for sprinkling

1 tablespoon paprika or smoked paprika

1 teaspoon minced fresh thyme

1 teaspoon minced fresh rosemary

4 garlic cloves, minced

TIP

It's recommended to test your oven's temperature beforehand. Preheat the oven to 500°F and check with a temperature gauge. Then turn the oven off and check the temperature after one hour to make sure it's at least 200°F, as some ovens have a self-cooling mechanism that will drop the temperature too low.

Prime rib is an intimidating cut of beef. It's also expensive, so you sure don't want to mess it up! However, we've got an easy recipe, and we're not lying when we say it's foolproof. Whether it's a special occasion or you've just got a hankering for some great beef, this is the recipe you need. We rub it with an herbed butter that will melt as it cooks for a tasty coating. The oven does all the hard work. I know you'll want to peek, but resist the urge to look until it's done! We do recommend checking that your oven temperature is accurate beforehand, because that will affect the cooking.

—◆—

1. Preheat the oven to 500°F. Let the roast sit at room temperature for about 1½ to 2 hours. This will ensure even cooking.

2. In a small bowl, whisk the butter with all the remaining ingredients until smooth.

3. Rub the roast with the seasoned butter so it is evenly coated on all sides. Place the roast, rib side down, in a large roasting pan. Generously sprinkle the top with more sea salt.

4. Roast for 25 to 30 minutes (5 minutes per pound), then turn the oven off. Let the roast sit in the oven for 2 hours—do not open the oven door during this time.

5. Remove the roast from the oven and check the temperature; it should read between 120°F and 125°F. Lightly cover with foil and let rest for 5 to 10 minutes. During this time, the internal temperature will rise slightly to bring it to medium rare, roughly 130°F. Slice against the grain and serve warm.

Green Chile–Pork Stew

PREP TIME: 30 minutes

TOTAL TIME: 1 hour and 35 minutes

MAKES 6 TO 8 SERVINGS

¾ cup all-purpose flour

2 teaspoons garlic powder

2 teaspoons ancho chile powder

½ teaspoon ground cumin

Salt and black pepper

3 to 4 pounds pork shoulder, trimmed and chopped into bite-sized pieces

½ cup vegetable oil

7 tomatillos, husked and cored

1 serrano chile, stemmed, seeded, and chopped

1 dried guajillo chile, stemmed, seeded, and chopped

1 yellow onion, sliced

2 garlic cloves, coarsely chopped

1 teaspoon dried cilantro or 2 teaspoons fresh

3¼ cups chicken broth

3 (4-ounce) cans whole green chiles, chopped

This classic south-of-the-border recipe starts with chunks of pork shoulder. We toss the meat in a little seasoned flour to enhance the flavor, and the flour also helps thicken the broth a bit as it simmers. Making your own green sauce with roasted tomatillos and serrano and guajillo chiles gives this stew a truly homemade taste. We've even taken the leftovers and served them for breakfast with our Easy Homemade Tortillas (page 110) and eggs. It's a versatile dish that will sure warm your heart and stomach.

———•◦•———

1. Preheat the oven to 400°F.

2. In a large bowl, combine the flour, garlic powder, ancho chile powder, cumin, and ½ teaspoon each salt and pepper. Add the pork and toss until well coated.

3. In a 12-inch cast-iron skillet heat ¼ cup of the oil over medium heat. Shaking off any excess flour, add half the pork to the skillet and cook, stirring occasionally, until lightly browned, about 5 minutes. Remove from the skillet and set aside. Heat the remaining ¼ cup oil and cook the remaining pork.

4. Meanwhile, place the tomatillos on a baking sheet and bake for about 15 minutes, until tender. Let cool slightly.

5. Add the tomatillos, serrano and guajillo chiles, onion, garlic, cilantro, and ¼ cup of the chicken broth to a blender. Blend until smooth.

TIP

If available, the Hatch brand of green chiles gives the best flavor.

6. Add the remaining 3 cups chicken broth and the green chiles to a large pot. Stir in the pork and the tomatillo sauce. Bring to a boil over high heat for 5 minutes, then reduce the heat to low, cover, and simmer for 45 minutes to 1 hour, until the pork is tender. Season with salt and pepper to taste, then serve.

Dogs, horses, and children all have great judgment when it comes to a man's character.

Traditional Pork Tamales

PREP TIME: **5 hours and 30 minutes**

TOTAL TIME: **7 hours and 30 minutes**

MAKES ABOUT 3 DOZEN

2 cups chicken broth

3 garlic cloves, minced

½ cup chopped white onion

1 teaspoon ground cumin

Salt and black pepper

2½ pounds pork butt

2 bay leaves

1 (16-ounce) bag corn husks

2¼ cups masa mix (masa harina) for tamales

3 cups lard or manteca (Mexican lard; see Tip)

Red Sauce (page 216)

Everyone loves a tamale. Yes, they are a little time consuming but sure not difficult, and so worth the effort. Pork butt is simmered in a slow cooker, mixed with an authentic red sauce, and placed on top of masa or corn dough that's spread on corn husks. Then the whole thing is rolled up and steamed until the masa easily releases from the husks. This truly is a family recipe, because it's more fun when the whole family gets involved to make them.

———— ◆◆ ————

1. Pour the chicken broth into a slow cooker and turn to high. Add the garlic, onion, cumin, and 1 teaspoon each salt and pepper.

2. Cut the pork into about 2-inch chunks. Season all sides well with salt and pepper and add to the slow cooker along with the bay leaves. Cover and cook on low for about 4½ to 5 hours, until tender.

3. Meanwhile, about 2 hours before the meat is done, submerge the corn husks in a clean sink or bowl filled with hot water. Put a plate on top to weight the husks down and let soak. Drain well before using.

4. When the pork is done, strain the meat from the broth over a bowl and let cool slightly. Reserve the broth (about 4 cups). Shred the meat with two forks and set aside in a warm place.

5. Meanwhile, in a large bowl, combine the masa mix and 1 teaspoon each salt and pepper.

The biggest mistake made in tamale-making is using a masa mixture that is too dry. Be sure to stir in enough lard and broth to get a wet consistency that is easy to spread but will still hold together. For a how-to video, see our YouTube channel (youtube.com/cowboykentrollins).

Manteca is Mexican lard and typically has a richer flavor.

6. In a small saucepan, melt the lard over medium heat. Stir 1 cup of the lard and 2½ cups of the reserved meat broth into the masa mixture. Stir in 3 to 4 tablespoons of the red sauce to taste.

7. Lightly flour your hands and begin working the dough. Continue adding the meat broth and lard, about ½ cup at a time, until you get a very moist consistency that will stick together but can be easily spread. You may not end up using all the lard and/or broth.

8. Pour the remaining red sauce into the pulled pork and stir to combine.

9. Place a corn husk on a work surface or hold in your hand smooth side up. Spoon about 2 tablespoons of the masa mixture onto the narrow end of the husk. Smooth the masa out to create a thin 4-x-5-inch layer. Spread about 2 tablespoons of the pork down the center of the masa.

10. Fold the husk over lengthwise to meet the opposite side and roll under. Fold the long end of the husk under at the bottom of the tamale. Repeat with the remaining husks and masa mixture. (You won't use all the husks.)

11. Place the tamales, folded end down, in a tamale steamer. Cover them with a few remaining corn husks to hold in the moisture. Cover with the lid and steam for 1½ to 2 hours. The tamales are done when they easily unroll and release from the husks. Let the tamales rest for 4 to 5 minutes after removing from the steamer, to release easier.

(recipe continues)

Red Sauce

PREP TIME: 5 minutes

TOTAL TIME: 20 minutes

MAKES ABOUT 1 CUP

3 dried guajillo chiles, stemmed and seeded

3 dried ancho chiles, stemmed and seeded

1 jalapeño, stemmed and seeded

1 serrano chile, stemmed and seeded

1 large white onion, halved

2 garlic cloves, peeled

1. Add all the ingredients to a medium saucepan. Cover with water and bring to a boil for about 15 minutes, or until the chiles and onion are tender. Let cool to room temperature.

2. Strain the contents from the water (discard the water), add to a blender, and blend until smooth. Strain the sauce to ensure it is smooth.

Chicken and Rice Casserole

PREP TIME: **15 minutes**

TOTAL TIME: **1 hour and 45 minutes**

MAKES 6 TO 8 SERVINGS

1 cup white rice

6 boneless, skinless chicken breast halves

⅓ cup chopped onion

⅓ cup chopped celery

⅓ cup chopped green bell pepper

2 garlic cloves, minced

Salt and black pepper

1 (10½-ounce) can cream of chicken soup

Tender chicken breasts and rice are baked together with celery, bell pepper, and onion in a creamy chicken soup broth for this easy, family-pleasing meal.

1. Preheat the oven to 350°F.

2. Pour the rice into a 12-inch cast-iron skillet or 9-x-13-inch casserole dish.

3. Place the chicken breasts on top and evenly scatter the onion, celery, bell pepper, and garlic around them. Season with salt and pepper to taste.

4. Pour the soup into a small saucepan and stir in 1½ soup cans water. Bring to a boil over high heat, stirring occasionally.

5. Pour the soup over the chicken and vegetables, cover with foil, and bake for 1 hour and 20 minutes, or until the rice is tender. Remove the foil and bake for another 10 minutes, or until the chicken is lightly browned. Serve.

Life is a lot like gravy; sometimes it just takes a little stirring to get it smoothed out.

Chicken Spaghetti Bake

PREP TIME: **40 minutes**
TOTAL TIME: **1 hour**
MAKES 6 TO 8 SERVINGS

1 (12-ounce) package spaghetti

1 teaspoon salt

2 large boneless, skinless chicken breast halves

2 tablespoons butter

1 green bell pepper, chopped

1 yellow onion, chopped

2 cups sliced mushrooms

1 (10½-ounce) can cream of mushroom soup

1 pound Velveeta cheese, cut into cubes

Parmesan cheese for sprinkling (optional)

Spaghetti is typically served with a red sauce. But we've got a different take, using Velveeta cheese and mushroom soup for extra creaminess. Simply serve with a salad and you've got an easy weeknight meal.

———— •••• ————

1. Break the spaghetti in half and prepare according to the package directions. Drain and set aside.

2. Meanwhile, fill a large saucepan halfway with water and bring to a boil. Stir in the salt and add the chicken breasts. Be sure the chicken is generously covered with water. Bring back to a boil, reduce the heat to low, and simmer for about 25 minutes, until cooked through. Remove the chicken and set on a cutting board. Reserve 1 cup of the broth. When cool enough to handle, skin the chicken and shred the meat. Rinse the saucepan to use later.

3. Preheat the oven to 350°F.

4. Melt the butter in a large cast-iron skillet. Add the bell pepper and onion and cook over medium heat, stirring occasionally, until tender, 8 to 10 minutes. Add the mushrooms and cook, stirring frequently, until they begin to release their juices, 2 to 3 minutes more.

5. In the large saucepan, whisk together the mushroom soup and the reserved 1 cup chicken broth. Add the Velveeta cheese and cook over medium heat, stirring frequently, until melted. Turn off the heat and stir in the vegetables, chicken, and spaghetti.

6. Scrape the mixture into a buttered 9-x-13-inch casserole dish and sprinkle with Parmesan, if using. Bake for 20 minutes, or until bubbling. Serve.

Chicken–Tater Tot Casserole

PREP TIME: **35 minutes**
TOTAL TIME: **1 hour and 5 minutes**
MAKES ABOUT 6 SERVINGS

1 teaspoon salt

2 boneless, skinless chicken breast halves

1 (10½-ounce) can cream of chicken soup

1 (10½-ounce) can cream of bacon soup

¾ cup milk

1 cup sour cream

2 (4-ounce) cans chopped green chiles

1 (1-ounce) package ranch seasoning mix

2 cups shredded cheddar cheese

1 (2-pound) bag frozen Tater Tots

5 slices thick-cut bacon, cooked and chopped

This is a favorite of the grandkids, and if that isn't a selling point, I don't know what is! A great casserole dish to throw together on a weekday night, it will satisfy even the pickiest of eaters. Tater Tots, bacon, and chicken are baked in a sauce of cream of chicken and cream of bacon soup.

———◆◆◆———

1. Fill a large saucepan halfway with water and bring to a boil. Stir in the salt and add the chicken breasts. Be sure the chicken is generously covered with water. Bring back to a boil, reduce the heat to low, and simmer for about 25 minutes, until cooked through. Remove from the water. When cool enough to handle, chop.

2. Preheat the oven to 350°F. Lightly butter a 12-inch cast-iron skillet or 9-x-13-inch casserole dish.

3. In a large bowl, whisk together the chicken soup, bacon soup, milk, sour cream, green chiles, and ranch mix. Stir in the chicken, cheese, and Tater Tots until well coated.

4. Scrape the mixture into the skillet or dish and top with the chopped bacon. Bake for about 30 minutes, until heated through. Serve.

Southern-Style Fried Chicken

PREP TIME: **2 hours and 45 minutes**

TOTAL TIME: **3 hours and 15 minutes**

MAKES ABOUT 6 SERVINGS

1 (3½- to 4-pound) whole chicken

2¼ cups buttermilk

1 tablespoon baking powder

2¼ cups all-purpose flour

⅓ cup cornstarch

2 tablespoons black pepper

1 tablespoon poultry seasoning

1 tablespoon onion powder

1 tablespoon garlic powder

2 teaspoons paprika or smoked paprika

2 teaspoons white pepper

1½ teaspoons seasoned salt

1½ teaspoons lemon pepper

1 teaspoon celery salt

1 teaspoon cayenne pepper (optional)

Peanut oil, canola oil, or lard for frying

This Southern specialty starts with a buttermilk bath mixed with a dab of baking powder, which is going to help make that crust pop. Be sure you let the yardbird soak for at least 2 hours in the refrigerator to tenderize it. Have a lid handy for your skillet, because that really helps create even cooking and a better crust. Lard gives the best flavor.

———◆———

1. Cut the legs and wings from the chicken. Separate the thighs from the drumsticks by cutting through the joint. Cut the breast into 4 equal pieces.

2. In a large bowl or casserole dish, whisk together the buttermilk and baking powder. Add the chicken pieces and turn to generously coat. Cover and refrigerate for 2 hours.

3. Remove the chicken from the refrigerator and flip each piece over in the buttermilk. Cover and let rest at room temperature for 30 minutes.

4. Meanwhile, in a medium bowl, combine the flour, cornstarch, and spices.

5. Add about 1½ cups of the flour mixture to a zippertop bag. With tongs, remove a piece of chicken from the buttermilk and allow any excess buttermilk to drip off. Place the chicken in the bag and toss to generously coat. Place on a wire rack. Repeat with the remaining chicken, adding more flour mixture to the bag as needed. Let the chicken sit for 10 minutes before frying.

6. In a large cast-iron skillet pour in the oil to reach about hallway up the side and heat to between 340°F and 350°F. Add the chicken a few pieces at a time, cover with a lid, and

When checking the internal temperature, be sure to probe at the thickest part of the chicken.

If you don't have a lid for your cast skillet, you can use another skillet flipped over as a lid.

fry for 5 to 8 minutes, until a light golden brown underneath. Remove the lid and flip each piece. Continue cooking, without the lid and turning as needed, for another 5 to 7 minutes, until the chicken is an even golden brown and the internal temperature is 165°F. Let cool slightly on a paper towel or wire rack before serving.

Salmon Patties with Dill Sauce

PREP TIME: 10 minutes

TOTAL TIME: 25 minutes

MAKES TEN TO TWELVE 2½-INCH PATTIES

¾ cup all-purpose flour

1 teaspoon baking powder

1 (14.75-ounce) can pink salmon

2 large eggs, beaten

⅓ cup finely chopped green onions

Salt and black pepper

Peanut or canola oil for frying

Dill Sauce (below)

Now, this is comfort food! Canned salmon, which has a bolder flavor than fresh-caught, is combined with green onions and seasoned flour, and the crispy patties are pan-fried. When they're paired with our homemade dill sauce, you'll never know these little fellers didn't come straight from the river!

———◆◆◆———

1. In a small bowl, combine the flour and baking powder.

2. Pour the salmon, with the juice from the can, into a medium bowl. Using a fork, break up the salmon and remove any bones. Stir in the eggs, green onions, and salt and pepper to taste. Slowly stir in the flour mixture.

3. In a large cast-iron skillet, heat about ½ inch of oil to 350°F.

4. Take 2 to 3 tablespoons of the mixture and place it in the skillet. Slightly mash down to create about a 2½-inch-wide patty. Add a few at a time to the skillet and fry for 2 to 3 minutes per side, until golden brown. Let cool slightly on a paper towel or wire rack. Serve with the dill sauce.

PREP TIME: 2 minutes

TOTAL TIME: 32 minutes

MAKES 1 CUP

½ cup sour cream

½ cup mayonnaise

1 teaspoon lemon juice

1 teaspoon dried dill

¼ teaspoon garlic powder

Dill Sauce

Combine all the ingredients in a small bowl. Cover and refrigerate for 30 minutes, or until ready to serve.

Rosemary-Baked Trout

PREP TIME: **10 minutes**
TOTAL TIME: **30 minutes**
MAKES 4 SERVINGS

1 stick butter, melted

4 trout, cleaned

Lemon pepper

Coarse sea salt

2 lemons, sliced

Olive oil

Leaves from 1 large rosemary sprig, chopped

Glaze (below)

OUTDOOR COOKING TIP

When cooking in a Dutch oven with coals, after baking the fish for 8 to 10 minutes, remove the heat from the bottom of the oven and finish baking with top heat only.

I like to bake trout on a layer of lemon slices to keep it from burning. I top the fish with more lemon slices and fresh chopped rosemary before baking, then drizzle a mix of honey, rosemary, and garlic over the fish toward the end of baking to make a glaze. This is a great recipe to make in cast iron while camping too.

1. Preheat the oven to 375°F. Pour the butter into a 12-inch cast-iron skillet or 9-x-13-inch baking dish.

2. Season the fish inside and out with lemon pepper and sea salt. Place 2 or 3 lemon slices inside each fish.

3. Place about 3 lemon slices per fish in the bottom of the skillet or dish. Lay each trout on top of the lemons, then drizzle with olive oil and sprinkle with rosemary.

4. Bake about 15 minutes, or until the fish is white and flaky. Spread the glaze over the fish and bake for another 3 minutes. Serve warm.

PREP TIME: **5 minutes**
TOTAL TIME: **5 minutes**
MAKES ABOUT ¼ CUP

2 garlic cloves, minced

2 tablespoons honey

2 teaspoons minced rosemary

2 teaspoons olive oil

1 teaspoon lemon juice

Glaze

Whisk all the ingredients together in a small bowl. Spread over the trout.

Poor Man's Lobster

PREP TIME: **10 minutes**

TOTAL TIME: **15 minutes**

MAKES 4 SERVINGS

12 cups water

½ lemon, cut into 4 pieces

1 cup sugar

2 pounds halibut or cod fillets, thawed if frozen and at room temperature

Lemon juice

Dill seed or dried dill

Melted butter for serving

Lobster is delicious, but it sure ain't cheap! We create an imitation by boiling white fish in sugar water, which brings out a rich flavor that nearly tastes like lobster. Dip in melted butter and serve as an appetizer or main course.

1. Bring the water to a boil in a large pot. Add the lemon pieces and sugar and stir until the sugar dissolves. Boil for 2 to 3 minutes.

2. Rinse the fish well and cut into 1-inch chunks. Add to the pot and boil, without stirring, until the chunks begin bobbing and float to the top, 4 to 5 minutes. Remove with a slotted spoon and let cool slightly on a wire rack or paper towel.

3. Sprinkle with lemon juice and dill and serve with melted butter for dipping.

TIP

Halibut holds up when boiling, or you can use cod. This also works with white freshwater fish, such as walleye, perch, or crappie.

Cowboy Cajun Shrimp Étouffée

PREP TIME: 30 minutes

TOTAL TIME: 55 minutes

MAKES 6 TO 8 SERVINGS

1 stick butter

2 yellow onions, chopped

2 celery stalks, chopped

1 green bell pepper, chopped

1 poblano chile, roasted (see Tip) and chopped

4 garlic cloves, minced

Salt and black pepper

¼ cup all-purpose flour

2 cups chicken broth

¼ cup white wine

2 pounds large uncooked shrimp, peeled, deveined, and thawed if frozen

Rice or bread for serving

This cowboy is going down to the bayou! Étouffée *means "to smother," and we are sure going to do that. In this classic Cajun recipe, shrimp are simmered in a thick sauce of onions, celery, green bell pepper, and garlic, with a roasted poblano added for smoky flavor. Then I smother rice or bread with the étouffée. You can also add sliced spicy sausage or chorizo for a heartier dish. For a richer shrimp flavor, use red or rock shrimp.*

1. Melt the butter in a 12-inch cast-iron skillet or stew pot over medium heat. Stir in the onions, celery, bell pepper, poblano, and garlic and cook, stirring occasionally, until the vegetables are soft and lightly browned, 20 to 30 minutes. Season with salt and pepper to taste.

2. Sprinkle in the flour and cook, stirring occasionally, until slightly thickened, about 3 minutes.

3. Stir in the chicken broth, wine, and shrimp and cook, stirring occasionally, until the shrimp are pink and opaque, about 15 minutes. Serve warm over rice or bread.

TIP

To roast a pepper, place it over a flame with tongs, turning frequently, until it blisters and evenly chars. Place the pepper in a plastic bag with 1 tablespoon cold water and seal. Let sit for a few minutes. Remove the pepper from the bag and peel off the skin. The steam helps release the skin easier.

Crispy Cornmeal-Crusted Catfish

PREP TIME: **10 minutes**

TOTAL TIME: **20 minutes**

MAKES 6 TO 8 SERVINGS

2 cups cornmeal

⅔ cup all-purpose flour

1 tablespoon lemon pepper

1 tablespoon seasoned salt

2 tablespoons cornstarch

2 teaspoons baking powder

2 tablespoons buttermilk powder (see Tip)

2 cups warm water

6 to 8 large catfish fillets, thawed if frozen

Peanut or canola oil for frying

A cornmeal crust is traditional, but half the time it ends up falling off before you even get to wrap a lip around it. A mix of buttermilk powder and cornstarch keeps the batter on the catfish for a crispy bite. This batter can also be used for a crunchy crust on other fried foods. When buying catfish, look for the cleanest and whitest fillets you can find, with no red or brown streaks. Try this with Chipotle Aioli Sauce (page 163).

1. In a medium bowl, combine the cornmeal, flour, lemon pepper, and seasoned salt.

2. In a small bowl, combine the cornstarch, baking powder, buttermilk powder, and warm water.

3. Cut the catfish fillets into thirds and pat dry with a paper towel. Dip the fish into the wet mixture and then dredge through the cornmeal mixture to evenly coat. Repeat for a double coating.

4. In a large, deep saucepan or Dutch oven, heat 3 to 4 inches of oil to 350°F. Deep-fry the catfish, turning as needed, until the crust is golden brown and crispy, 4 to 5 minutes. Let cool slightly on a paper towel or wire rack. Serve.

TIP

Buttermilk powder can be found online or sometimes in the supermarket. Or, if you don't have any, replace the water with 2 cups buttermilk.

The Last Gate

Dessert

When I was young, I remember riding with Pa in the pickup and pulling up to an old barbed wire gate to the entrance of a pasture. It was held together with rusty baling wire and a few staves to hold it up off the ground. It was tethered to the gatepost with a piece of nylon rope that was frayed and looked like it had been tied a million times. I didn't know how the old thing could withstand a mess of tumbleweeds, much less some old range cow.

Pa asked, "Reckon you could open that gate? It's a mite tricky to untie."

I got out and proceeded to untie the square knot half-hitched configuration. It took me a while, but I finally got it untied and dragged the gate out of the way. When he pulled through, I asked, "Do I shut it?"

He responded, "That's the way we found it, ain't it?"

You see, that's cowboy etiquette. You always leave the gate as you found it. Part of the reason for that is because even though there might not be a cow in sight, they'll find an open gate. A cow doesn't have ESP, she has TLGO (they left the gate open) radar.

There were two more gates to go through on our way to go fix a windmill, and all were a challenge to open and shut. This windmill was an oasis to any four-legged or winged creature within three hundred acres.

We headed deeper into the pasture and closer to the banks of the Red River. "What are we doing now?" I asked Pa. "I thought we were through."

"Not hardly. We've got more gates to go through, fences to mend, and cows to check," he answered.

I finally asked him, "Why are there so many gates? Couldn't we just get by with one?"

He told me, "We have to separate pastures for better grazing. It's just like your mama's cooking. She doesn't cook all three meals at one time, she spreads them out over breakfast, dinner, and supper. We'd run out of groceries if we ate them all at once. Just like those cows getting to graze in a new green pasture, we can look forward not only to the meal at hand but Mama's desserts that follow."

A day goes by faster when you're working with someone special and doing what you love. But as the sun was fading into the western sky, so was I. It seemed like I had walked a thousand miles and opened hundreds of gates. Pa looked at me and said, "Been a long day for a little feller, hasn't it?"

"Sure has," I answered, "but I bet Mama has supper fixed, and I sure am hungry!"

As we headed home and finally reached the last gate, I asked him, "You sure this is the last one?"

He grinned and said, "Nope, you got one more thing to open, and that's the front door back home." The smell of Mama's kitchen greeted us as we walked in. The table was set, family members were gathered, and we blessed it.

We hope as you enter into this final pasture full of desserts, you find the grazing to be satisfying.

———◦•◦———

Cranberry-Coconut Cookies

PREP TIME: **10 minutes**
TOTAL TIME: **25 minutes**
MAKES ABOUT 15 COOKIES

1¾ cups all-purpose flour, plus more for dusting

½ teaspoon baking powder

1 stick butter, softened

1 cup sugar

¾ cup chopped fresh cranberries

½ heaping cup shredded sweetened coconut

1 large egg

1 tablespoon grated orange zest

½ teaspoon almond extract

This is my favorite cookie of all time. It's perfect for the holidays and great for a Christmas cookie exchange. Tangy chopped cranberries are mixed with shredded coconut, orange zest, and almond extract for satisfying flavor in every bite. They bake up soft and thick.

1. Preheat the oven to 350°F with a rack in the middle.

2. In a medium bowl, mix together the flour and baking powder.

3. In a large bowl, using an electric mixer, cream together the butter and sugar until light and fluffy. Whisk in the cranberries, coconut, egg, orange zest, and almond extract.

4. Slowly mix the flour mixture into the wet mixture until combined.

5. Lightly flour your hands and form the dough into 15 balls the size of a golf ball. Place on an ungreased baking sheet about 1 inch apart and press down lightly in the middle of each ball to flatten slightly.

6. Bake for 12 to 15 minutes, until the bottoms are light golden brown. Be careful not to overbake to keep the cookies soft. Remove from the sheet and let cool slightly on a wire rack before serving.

Caramel-Pecan Cracker Bars

PREP TIME: **15 minutes**

TOTAL TIME: **1 hour and 30 minutes**

MAKES 9 SQUARES

1 sleeve saltine crackers

2 sticks butter

2 cups packed light brown sugar

⅔ cup crushed Ritz crackers

½ cup semisweet chocolate chips

½ cup peanut butter chips

½ cup chopped pecans

Saltine crackers are layered in a caramel sauce, topped with chocolate and peanut butter chips, then sprinkled with chopped pecans. Every chewy bite is salty and sweet.

1. Preheat the oven to 350°F with a rack in the middle. Line an 8-x-8-inch square baking dish with foil and lightly butter the foil.

2. Arrange half the saltine crackers in a single layer in the dish. Break any crackers or overlap them to fit. Set aside.

3. For the caramel sauce, melt the butter in a medium saucepan over medium heat. Stir in the brown sugar and bring to a boil, stirring constantly, for 2 to 3 minutes, until the sugar has melted.

4. Pour half the caramel sauce over the crackers. Top with the rest of the saltines, then evenly pour over the remaining sauce. Sprinkle with the Ritz crackers.

5. Bake for 7 minutes. Remove the dish from the oven and turn the oven off. Top the dish with the chocolate and peanut butter chips, return it to the oven, and let sit for 8 minutes, or until the chips have melted.

6. Remove the dish from the oven and lightly smooth the softened chips with a spatula. Sprinkle with the nuts and pat down gently. Let cool completely. Cut into squares and serve.

"Reindeer Poop"

PREP TIME: **10 minutes**
TOTAL TIME: **15 minutes**
MAKES ABOUT 15 CLUSTERS

1 cup sugar
1 cup light corn syrup
1 cup smooth peanut butter
5 cups Cocoa Puffs cereal

TIP

These go fast, so you may want to make a double batch! A 20-ounce cereal box will do a double recipe.

For these crunchy, gooey treats, Cocoa Puffs cereal is mixed with peanut butter and sugar. The clusters are delicious throughout the year but a must at Christmas.

1. In a large saucepan, whisk together the sugar and corn syrup. Bring to a light boil over medium-high heat, stirring frequently, until the sugar dissolves, 3 to 5 minutes.

2. Remove from the heat and whisk in the peanut butter until smooth. Stir in the cereal until evenly coated.

3. Scoop heaping tablespoonfuls of the mixture (about fifteen 2-inch clusters) onto waxed paper. Let cool to room temperature. Serve. Store in a covered container for up to 5 days.

Out here we don't have Wi-Fi. We connect with friends and family over a good cup of coffee.

The Last Sortin'

We all watched and waited
As the good Lord sorted stock.
He was carefully picking and
choosing
As He stood on the solid rock.

He was checking brands
As they came to the pearly gates.
He controlled their destiny
And it was He who held their fate.

Some were worn and weary,
Others blind and lame.
Young and old alike,
They all cried out His name.

The Saints pushed each one
Down an alley made of gold.
There they stood in silence
As their tally book was told.

Some were guided toward the light
While others were cast aside.
Never to be seen again,
Into the darkness they would ride.

Some brands were very visible
And others were hard to see.
Then I began to wonder,
Had my life made the right mark on me?

Had I helped my neighbor?
Had I always been fair?
Did I choose kindness and love
Over hate and despair?

Was I branded with the blood
That was shed for me?
The everlasting promise of life
From the cross at Calvary?

With each one I got closer
And finally it was my time.
Then the Lord said, "Let him in.
This one is one of mine."

Irish Cream Truffles

PREP TIME: **1 hour and 10 minutes**
TOTAL TIME: **1 hour and 20 minutes**
MAKES ABOUT 18 TRUFFLES

¼ cup heavy cream

1 (12-ounce) bag milk chocolate chips

3 tablespoons Irish cream liqueur

Sprinkles, powdered sugar, or crushed nuts for topping

Shannon makes these to celebrate St. Patrick's Day. You know the Irish: Shan adds Irish cream liqueur for a hint of nutty creaminess, which is blended with rich milk chocolate. You could also make them with semisweet or dark chocolate, if you prefer. Dress these up with powdered sugar, sprinkles, or nuts, or leave them plain.

———— ◆ ————

1. Set up a double boiler by filling a saucepan halfway with water and placing it over high heat. When the water begins to boil, set a heatproof medium bowl over the saucepan (don't let the bottom of the bowl touch the boiling water). Warm the cream in the bowl, then stir in the chocolate chips and cook, stirring frequently, until the chips have melted. (The steam will slowly melt the chips, without scorching or burning.)

2. Remove from the heat and whisk in the liqueur until smooth. Cover and refrigerate for about 1 hour, until semifirm.

3. Put about 1 tablespoon of the chocolate mixture in your hand and quickly form into a ball. The warmth of your hands will cause the truffles to melt, so you want to do this as quickly as possible. Roll the ball in sprinkles, sugar, or crushed nuts, if desired. Repeat with the remaining chocolate mixture and toppings. If the truffles become too tacky to handle, you can rechill the chocolate for about 10 minutes. Serve chilled or at room temperature.

Stand firm in the faith; be courageous; be strong.

—Corinthians 16:13

Mocha Chocolate Mousse

PREP TIME: **15 minutes**

TOTAL TIME: **45 minutes**

MAKES 4 TO 5 SERVINGS

1 cup heavy cream

⅓ cup plus 2 tablespoons sugar

1 teaspoon vanilla extract

1 tablespoon unsweetened cocoa powder

2 large egg whites

1 tablespoon instant coffee powder or grounds

Berries for serving (optional)

Before meeting Shan, the only mousse I was familiar with had antlers. This has a light, pudding-like texture with the perfect pairing of cocoa powder and a hint of coffee. You'll want to lick it right out of the bowl.

———•••———

1. In a medium bowl, using an electric mixer, beat the cream, ⅓ cup of the sugar, and the vanilla until stiff. Beat in the cocoa powder. Clean the beaters.

2. In another medium bowl, beat the egg whites and instant coffee until stiff. Beat in the remaining 2 tablespoons sugar until smooth.

3. Fold the egg white mixture into the cream mixture and refrigerate until chilled, about 30 minutes. Serve with berries, if desired.

Cowboy Crown Crème Brûlée

PREP TIME: **25 minutes**
TOTAL TIME: **1 hour and 15 minutes**
MAKES 6 SERVINGS

2 cups heavy cream

½ cup mascarpone cheese (see headnote)

¼ cup whiskey

4 teaspoons vanilla extract

¼ cup plus 6 teaspoons sugar

6 large egg yolks

½ cup honey

Right here is about as fancy as the cowboy is going to get. If you've never had crème brûlée, it's like a rich pudding, but what makes it special is the crackling crust. A topping of sugar is heated and caramelized to crispness. The pudding has a rich egg custard base, with mascarpone for extra creaminess. You can substitute ½ cup cream cheese, but mascarpone gives a deeper flavor. Then I add vanilla and whiskey (we prefer Crown Royal). Be sure to chill this well and then indulge!

1. Preheat the oven to 325°F with a rack in the middle. Butter six 8-ounce ramekins.

2. In a medium saucepan, warm the cream over medium-high heat. Stir in the mascarpone, whiskey, vanilla, and ¼ cup of the sugar and bring to a boil, whisking constantly. Remove from the heat and let sit for 15 minutes.

3. Meanwhile, in a medium bowl, beat the egg yolks and honey until frothy. Slowly whisk in the cream mixture, then pour the custard into the ramekins.

4. Place the ramekins in a baking pan and add hot water to the pan until it reaches halfway up the ramekins. Bake for 45 to 50 minutes, until the custards are mostly set but still a little jiggly in the middles. Remove the ramekins from the water bath, cover, and refrigerate for at least 2 hours or up to 3 days.

5. Just before serving, sprinkle 1 teaspoon sugar on top of each custard. With a culinary torch on high, heat the sugar until a crisp, dark golden brown crust forms. Serve.

TIP

Using a culinary torch is the best method; however, if you don't have one, set the ramekins on a baking sheet and place directly under the oven broiler at 500°F. Broil for about 1 minute, rotating frequently, until an even crust forms. Watch carefully so you don't burn them.

'Naner Pudding

PREP TIME: 30 minutes
TOTAL TIME: 50 minutes
MAKES ABOUT 8 SERVINGS

1½ cups heavy cream

½ cup sugar

1 cup milk

1 (5-ounce) package instant vanilla pudding mix

1 (14-ounce) can sweetened condensed milk

6 or 7 large ripe bananas

1 (11-ounce) box vanilla wafers

This dessert is the holy grail of Southern desserts and can be found at nearly every reunion, potluck, or family get-together. My favorite part of this pudding is the creamy, thick texture. You can get creative in the number of layers and types of dishes to serve this in.

1. In a medium bowl, using an electric mixer, beat the cream and sugar until stiff. Cover and refrigerate.

2. In a large bowl, beat the milk, pudding mix, and condensed milk until slightly thickened, about 5 minutes.

3. In a small bowl, mash 1 banana with a fork until smooth. Beat into the pudding mixture. Cover and refrigerate for about 20 minutes, or until it reaches a thick pudding consistency.

4. Meanwhile, thinly slice the remaining bananas.

5. Arrange half the vanilla wafers in an even layer in the bottom of a 9-x-13-inch baking pan.

6. Fold half the whipped cream into the pudding mixture. Evenly spoon the pudding mixture over the wafers, then layer with the sliced bananas and remaining whipped cream. Crush the remaining wafers and sprinkle them on top. Cover and refrigerate for 20 minutes, or until you are ready to serve.

Old-Fashioned Oatmeal Peach Cobbler

PREP TIME: 30 minutes
TOTAL TIME: 55 minutes
MAKES ABOUT 8 SERVINGS

1¼ cups packed light brown sugar

1¼ cups all-purpose flour

2 sticks plus 5 tablespoons butter, chilled

2 pounds fresh peaches, peeled and sliced, or 2 (15-ounce) cans peaches in heavy syrup

2 cups sugar (if using fresh peaches)

¼ cup cornstarch

¼ cup maple syrup

1½ cups old-fashioned oats

1 teaspoon ground cinnamon

1 teaspoon ground nutmeg

1 teaspoon salt

Ice cream for serving

My mother made this on special occasions. She always told us, "Any time you can get all the family together is a special occasion!" We had a couple peach trees, and Mama would boil fresh peaches down with a little sugar. She'd pour that mixture over a crust and drizzle with a little maple syrup for another layer of flavor. An oatmeal, cinnamon, and nutmeg crumble finishes this off, and it comes out of the oven a bubbling masterpiece.

1. Preheat the oven to 350°F with a rack in the middle. Butter a 12-inch cast-iron skillet or 9-x-13-inch baking dish.

2. In a medium bowl, combine ¾ cup of the brown sugar and 1 cup of the flour. Cut in 1½ sticks of the butter to a fine crumble with a fork. Work the dough with your hands to form a ball.

3. Pat the dough into the bottom of the skillet or baking dish. Bake for 15 minutes, or until the crust is set.

4. Add the peaches to a large saucepan with the sugar and ½ stick of the butter. If using canned peaches, omit the sugar. Bring to a boil. Stir in the cornstarch and cook over medium-high heat, stirring frequently, until the peaches thicken slightly, about 3 minutes.

5. Remove the skillet from the oven and pour the peaches over the crust. Evenly drizzle the maple syrup on top.

When baking in a Dutch oven with coals, as the crust begins to set up and brown lightly around the edges, add the peaches and topping. Finish with more heat on the lid and lighter coals around the bottom, since the bottom crust has already baked.

6. In a medium bowl, combine the oats, remaining ½ cup brown sugar and ¼ cup flour, the cinnamon, nutmeg, and salt. Cut in the remaining 5 tablespoons butter until crumbly.

7. Sprinkle the oatmeal mixture on top of the peaches. Return the skillet to the oven and bake for 25 minutes, or until bubbly and browned on top. Let cool slightly and serve warm with ice cream.

Anyone can lead, but it takes great faith to follow.

Brown Sugar Banana Bread

PREP TIME: **10 minutes**
TOTAL TIME: **55 minutes**
MAKES ONE 9-X-5-INCH LOAF

2 very ripe bananas

4 ounces cream cheese, softened

1 cup sugar

1 stick butter, melted

1¾ cups all-purpose flour

1½ teaspoons baking powder

½ teaspoon salt

½ teaspoon vanilla extract

2 tablespoons light brown sugar

¼ teaspoon ground cinnamon

Nothing says homemade like good old-fashioned 'naner bread. Just a few simple additions take a simple banana bread recipe to the next level. Cream cheese is mixed into the batter for a richer and more moist consistency. A combination of brown sugar and cinnamon is sprinkled on top before baking, to give a subtle crunch and burst of extra flavor. This makes the perfect companion to a cup of cowboy coffee.

1. Preheat the oven to 350°F with a rack in the middle. Butter a 9-x-5-inch loaf pan.

2. In a large bowl, using an electric mixer, cream together the bananas, cream cheese, and sugar until smooth. Mix in the butter.

3. In a medium bowl, combine the flour, baking powder, and salt. With the mixer on low, slowly mix the flour mixture into the banana mixture. Whisk in the vanilla. Scrape the batter into the loaf pan.

4. In a small bowl, combine the brown sugar and cinnamon. Sprinkle the mixture evenly over the batter.

5. Bake for about 45 minutes, until an inserted toothpick comes out clean. Let cool to warm, then run a knife around the sides and turn the bread out of the pan. Invert and serve.

Cherry Macaroon Cake

PREP TIME: **10 minutes**
TOTAL TIME: **50 minutes**
MAKES ABOUT 12 SERVINGS

1 (16-ounce) box angel food cake mix

⅓ cup sugar

1½ cups shredded sweetened coconut, plus more for topping

3 large eggs

1 cup heavy cream

1 teaspoon vanilla extract

1 teaspoon coconut extract

2 (21-ounce) cans cherry pie filling

2 teaspoons almond extract

A macaroon is one of my favorite cookies, and my favorite cake growing up was angel food. So, I decided to blend the two into an easy skillet bake that combines the chewy coconut characteristics of a macaroon and the light airiness of angel food. For more color and flavor, we top this with cherry pie filling, but you could sure use with any pie filling or fruit combination you'd like.

1. Preheat the oven to 350°F with a rack in the middle. Butter and flour a 12-inch cast-iron skillet or 9-x-13-inch baking pan.

2. In a large bowl, whisk together the cake mix, sugar, and coconut.

3. In a medium bowl, whisk together the eggs, cream, vanilla, and coconut extract.

4. Add the egg mixture to the cake mixture and whisk until smooth. Pour the batter into the skillet or pan and bake for about 40 minutes, until the crust sets up and an inserted toothpick comes out clean.

5. Meanwhile, in a small bowl, combine the cherries and almond extract.

6. Remove the cake from the oven and let cool to room temperature. Spread the cherries on top, sprinkle with coconut, and serve.

Aunt Ola's Chocolate Cake

PREP TIME: **10 minutes**
TOTAL TIME: **35 minutes**
MAKES 12 SERVINGS

2½ cups all-purpose flour

2 cups sugar

5 tablespoons unsweetened cocoa powder

1 teaspoon baking powder

¼ teaspoon salt

1 cup buttermilk

1 cup vegetable oil

2 large eggs

2 teaspoons baking soda

1 cup hot water

1 teaspoon vanilla extract

Chocolate Icing (page 256)

Just simple chocolatey goodness right here, folks. This was the first cake that I ever made, at the age of nine. I remember standing on a stool and my mother guiding me through the process of baking the best chocolate cake I had ever tasted. And the bonus was I got to lick the beaters clean. My Aunt Ola was a great cook, and her cake was served at every family birthday. It has an old-fashioned chocolate flavor and bakes up super moist. The best part is the chocolate icing: Poured over while the cake is still warm, it cools to a rich and gooey topping.

1. Preheat the oven to 350°F with a rack in the middle. Butter and flour a 12-inch cast-iron skillet or 9-x-13-inch baking pan.

2. In a large bowl, combine the flour, sugar, cocoa, baking powder, and salt.

3. In a medium bowl, whisk together the buttermilk, oil, and eggs. Dissolve the baking soda in the hot water and whisk into the buttermilk mixture.

4. Whisk the wet mixture into the flour mixture until smooth, then whisk in the vanilla.

5. Pour the batter into the skillet or pan and bake for about 25 minutes, until an inserted toothpick comes out clean. Let cool on a wire rack. Top with the icing while the cake is still warm.

(recipe continues)

Chocolate Icing

PREP TIME: 10 minutes
TOTAL TIME: 10 minutes
MAKES ABOUT 2½ CUPS

1½ cups sugar

3 tablespoons unsweetened cocoa powder

¾ cup milk

½ stick butter

1 teaspoon vanilla extract

1. While the cake is cooling, combine the sugar and cocoa powder in a small saucepan. Whisk in the milk. Bring to a low boil over medium-high heat, stirring frequently.

2. Add the butter and vanilla and continue cooking until the butter has melted, stirring frequently. Turn the heat to high and bring to a boil for about 4 minutes, stirring constantly. To test if the icing has boiled long enough, place a drop of it into a cup of cold water. If it forms a ball, it's done. However, if it splatters at the bottom of the cup, continue boiling until a ball forms when tested.

3. Pour over the still-warm cake and smooth out with a spatula. Let the icing and cake cool completely before cutting and serving.

Cranberry-Orange Cheesecake

PREP TIME: **10 minutes**

TOTAL TIME: **3 hours and 40 minutes**

MAKES **8 SERVINGS**

2 (8-ounce) packages cream cheese, softened

⅔ cup plus ¼ cup sugar

2 large eggs

2 teaspoons vanilla extract

1 (9-inch) store-bought graham cracker crust or homemade (see page 260), baked

1 navel orange

2 cups fresh cranberries

We start off with a classic creamy cheesecake, but to jazz it up we finish it with a lightly sweetened topping of orange and cranberries. This is to serve during the holidays for a festive and colorful dessert.

———— •••• ————

1. Preheat the oven to 350°F with a rack in the middle.

2. In a large bowl, using an electric mixer, cream together the cream cheese and ⅔ cup of the sugar until smooth. Beat in the eggs and vanilla until smooth.

3. Pour the batter into the crust and bake for 20 minutes. Place a crust saver or shield or a piece of foil over the crust and bake for another 10 minutes. Let cool on a wire rack, then refrigerate for at least 3 hours, or until the middle of the cake has set.

4. Meanwhile, grate 2 teaspoons of zest from the orange. Peel the orange and discard the peels.

5. Add the whole orange, cranberries, remaining ¼ cup sugar, and orange zest to a food processor or blender. Process or blend until finely chopped. Transfer to a bowl, cover, and refrigerate for 1 hour. When ready to serve, drain any excess liquid from the cranberries and spoon them on top of the cheesecake. Serve.

TIP

Be sure to drain all the moisture from the fruit before topping so the cheesecake doesn't become soggy.

Indian Fry Bread

PREP TIME: **2 hours and 10 minutes**

TOTAL TIME: **2 hours and 15 minutes**

MAKES 10 FRY BREADS

4 cups all-purpose flour, plus more for dusting

2 tablespoons baking powder

1 teaspoon salt

1½ to 2 cups warm water

3 tablespoons vegetable oil, plus more for frying

½ stick butter, melted

Honey and powdered sugar for topping

The past is like horse wrecks and homework— thanks for the lessons!

This soft bread with a rich, buttery flavor will transport you back to your favorite fair. The dough is very simple, but the secret is to let it rest for 2 hours. It's a must to top this off with powdered sugar and honey. You can also take this dish a step further and serve it up for the main course, with our recipe for Indian Tacos on page 209.

1. In a large bowl, combine the flour, baking powder, and salt. Stir in 1½ cups of the warm water and the oil just until combined. With your hands, begin working the dough. You may need to slowly add more water to create a soft and slightly tacky dough. Cover and let rest in a warm place for 2 hours.

2. Pour the butter over the dough and knead for 2 minutes. Pinch off the dough to make ten 2½- to 3-inch balls. Roll the balls out to thin 7- to 8-inch circles on a lightly floured surface.

3. In a large saucepan or Dutch oven, heat 3 to 4 inches of oil to 350°F. Shake off any excess flour from one of the dough circles and deep-fry, turning once, until a light golden brown, about 2 minutes per side. Repeat with remaining dough circles. Cool slightly on a paper towel or wire rack. Top with honey and powdered sugar and serve immediately.

Strawboffee Pie

PREP TIME: 20 minutes

TOTAL TIME: 2 hours 20 minutes

MAKES 8 SERVINGS

1½ cups finely crushed graham crackers

¼ cup powdered sugar

⅛ teaspoon salt

2 sticks butter, melted

½ cup packed dark brown sugar

1 (14-ounce) can sweetened condensed milk

1½ cups heavy cream

½ cup sugar

2 heaping cups stemmed and sliced fresh strawberries

Grated chocolate for topping (optional)

Shannon brought this dessert all the way from Northern Ireland to share it with y'all. A graham cracker crust lays the foundation for a thick filling of toffee to rest upon. A generous portion of sliced strawberries and thick homemade whipped cream tops it all off.

———— ••• ————

1. Preheat the oven to 375°F with a rack in the middle. Butter a 9-inch pie pan.

2. In a medium bowl, combine the graham crackers, powdered sugar, and salt. Stir in half the butter.

3. Evenly press the mixture into the pan and up the side. Bake for about 8 minutes, or until lightly toasted. Let cool on a wire rack.

4. For the toffee filling, pour the remaining butter into a medium saucepan. Stir in the brown sugar and cook over medium heat, stirring frequently, until the sugar has melted.

5. Stir in the condensed milk and bring to a boil for about 3 minutes, stirring constantly. Pour the toffee filling into the cooled pie crust. Cover and refrigerate for 2 hours.

6. In a medium bowl, using an electric mixer, beat the heavy cream and sugar until stiff.

7. Spread the strawberries over the toffee. Top with the whipped cream and grated chocolate (if desired) and serve, or refrigerate until ready to serve.

Homemade Cherry-Almond Ice Cream

PREP TIME: **30 minutes**

TOTAL TIME: **3 hours**

MAKES 1 GALLON

4 large eggs

2½ cups sugar

2 pints heavy cream

2 teaspoons vanilla extract

1 teaspoon almond extract

2 cups pitted and coarsely chopped dark sweet cherries

¾ cup sliced almonds

About 4 cups whole milk

Ice cubes

Rock salt

TIP

In the last step, you can also cover the bucket and cansister with an old towel for more insulation and a harder freeze.

A good homemade ice cream always takes me back to my childhood and warm Sunday afternoons. After church, folks all gathered under the shade of the porch and waited for someone to finish cranking on the old ice cream freezer. Our ice cream has almond extract, chunks of fresh dark sweet cherries, and almond slices for a little crunch. So, gather your crew and get to cranking!

1. Freeze the canister of your ice cream maker for at least 30 minutes.

2. Meanwhile, whisk the eggs well in a large bowl. Whisk in the sugar until thickened and smooth. Whisk in the cream and the vanilla and almond extracts. Stir in the cherries and almonds.

3. Pour the mixture into the chilled canister. Pour in the milk until it reaches the fill line in the canister.

4. Put the canister in the ice cream maker and freeze according to the manufacturer's directions by packing with ice and rock salt.

5. Plug in or crank for about 30 minutes, or until the motor stops and the ice cream is thick. Remove the dasher, seal the top of the canister with foil, and replace the lid. Cover the lid with more foil. Drain the water off the ice and repack the freezer bucket well with more ice and salt. Allow to set for about 2 hours or until hardened.

Index